SAN FRANCISCO
Like a
Local

SAN FRANCISCO
Like a Local

BY THE PEOPLE WHO CALL IT HOME

Contents

EAT

DRINK

SHOP

ARTS & CULTURE

NIGHTLIFE

OUTDOORS

meet the locals

MATT CHARNOCK

Caffeine addict Matt moved to the "seven-by-seven" – as the locals call SF – five years ago. Outside of drinking coffee, and editing and writing for a half-dozen Bay Area publications, Matt is running across the city's green spaces, quaffing drinks in dive bars, and perusing local farmers' markets (of which he is obsessed).

LAURA CHUBB

A native of northern England, Laura lived and worked in London, Dubai, and New York before settling on San Francisco, seduced by the sunny siren call of California. When not writing for a plethora of magazines and news outlets, Laura is tucking into NorCal fare and hiking up yet another hill to discover yet another breath-stealing view.

San Francisco

WELCOME TO THE CITY

Today, San Franciscans are divided into two camps: "old-school" (hippies) and "new-school" (techies). But if one thing unites them, it's the happy surety that living here makes them the luckiest people in the world. This widely held conviction might explain their "snobby" reputation. But if you lived here, you'd probably feel pretty self-satisfied, too. After all, San Franciscans are used to the best of everything: scenery, what with the city being surrounded on three sides by glittering water and muscular mountains; food and drink, thanks to the bounty of local farms, orchards, and vineyards; even sustainability (the city's green approach would make Greta Thunberg burst into applause).

Not that it's all plain sailing. The City by the Bay is no stranger to challenging times. Between earthquakes and dot-com crashes, residents have rebuilt the city several times over. And it always bounces back better than ever. And little

wonder; pioneering is in the blood. SF (only tourists say "San Fran") was built on the Gold Rush, and has blazed many a trail: LGBTQ+ rights, sharing economies, and revolutionary politics, to name a few. It's a small city with big ideas; a place where anything seems possible.

Some say the big tech invasion has tamed SF's subversive side. But scratch below the surface and you'll find free-thinking, flamboyant 'Frisco alive and kicking. And that's exactly where this book will take you. We know the places that San Franciscans adore, from experimental galleries housed in laundromat basements to the best live drag spaces. Of course, these pages can't capture every local's experience but instead offer a snapshot of the city's glorious diversity.

Whether you're a San Franciscan keen to rediscover your home, or a visitor looking for the bits that don't make it into guidebooks, we'll show you the real city. So strap in, and see SF like a local.

Liked by the locals

"The great joy of San Francisco is its contrasts: where ancient forest sits side by side with a city forging the future, and the excitement of a world-class capital meets the convenience and quirkiness of a small town."

LAURA CHUBB, JOURNALIST AND COPYWRITER

From joyful parades in the summer to festive fun in the winter, there's a cause for celebration with the dawn of each new season in San Francisco.

San Francisco
THROUGH THE YEAR

SPRING

STREET FOOD MARKETS
As the winter rain eases in March, locals start to brave the outdoors. Their reward? Top-notch food trucks and live entertainment on the Presidio's lawn, every Sunday.

PARADING IN THE STREET
Cultural celebrations draw SFers from all corners of the city into the streets. The party continues throughout spring, with Japantown Cherry Blossom Festival in April and the lively Carnaval in May.

BUFF STUFF
San Franciscans have a bit of a penchant for public nudity, and spring's forgiving climate offers an ideal opportunity to strip off. Naked runners take part in the Bay to Breakers Footrace; then bare-chested "messiahs" strut around Dolores Park in the Easter Hunky Jesus Contest.

SUMMER

PRIDE MONTH
Out-and-proud SFers and their allies fly rainbow flags at celebrations in June. The last Saturday of the month sees the Downtown Pride parade and community-driven Dyke March take to the streets, followed by a rowdy party at Dolores Park's Pride Picnic on the Sunday.

LIVE MUSIC
Outdoor stages spring up across the city for a summer of incredible live concerts. Fillmore Jazz Festival fills the streets with crooning tunes in July, while

Stern Grove Festival and Golden Gate Park's Outside Lands promise everything from folk to hip-hop in August.

ALFRESCO NIGHTS
Despite the evening chill, SFers are keen to linger outside during the summer. Picnics often turn into late-night BBQs, with friends toasting s'mores under the stars.

STREET FAIRS
Locals go nuts for street fairs in summer. Haight-Ashbury relives former glories with groovy tunes and tie-dye; North Beach offers up poetry readings; and the Mission's 20th Street Block Party is all about gourmet food and indie music.

FALL

SURF THE WAVES
San Franciscans gravitate toward the beach to cool off during the warmest season, especially in sultry September. Some suit-up to brave the waves, others prefer to kick back on the sand.

HARVEST TIME
Come fall, locals have one thing on their mind: a drive up to the Napa and Sonoma vineyards to raise a glass to the harvest. A weekend is often made of the occasion, with visits to pumpkin patches and corn mazes.

CITY OF LIGHTS
Families and friends head out for evening strolls over the Thanksgiving weekend, with eco-friendly light installations scattered across the city for Illuminate SF.

WINTER

THE GREAT OUTDOORS
Temperatures are mild and the skies generally clear in winter, so locals don their puffer vests and head out for scenic hikes around the city's coastal cliffs.

HOLIDAY CHEER
Come December, the holidays get a uniquely SF spin. Locals ice-skate in palm-tree-lined Union Square, don ugly sweaters for Downtown drinkathon SantaCon, and race in the Santa Skivvies Run (in their underwear, naturally).

WINTER TIPPLES
Spirits are kept high during the winter months with festivals devoted to grog, including January's Bay Area Brew Fest and February's SF Beer Week.

There's an art to being a San Franciscan, from the dos and don'ts when eating out to negotiating the city's streets. Here's a breakdown of all you need to know.

San Francisco
KNOW-HOW

For a directory of health and safety resources, safe spaces, and accessibility information, turn to page 190. For everything else, read on.

EAT

San Franciscans love nothing more than dining out. Weekends revolve around brunch, with cafés buzzing from 11am, whereas lunch is always a light, casual affair often eaten over a laptop. Dinner starts any time between 6 and 8pm and is the main meal of the day. Reservations are made months in advance, so book ahead wherever possible; alternatively line up 30 minutes before opening – it's your best shot at nabbing a walk-in table.

DRINK

San Franciscans take their coffee very seriously; we're talking specialist pours, not your standard Americano. As for alcohol, the city's drinking scene generally falls into two extremes: cheap dive bars and pricey, swanky spots. Californian wine is eye-wateringly expensive (about $14 a glass). Thankfully, two-hour happy hours, starting from around 5pm, are common and make things more affordable. Beer lovers, take note: craft beers are so strong that only half pints are allowed.

SHOP

By and large, San Franciscans prefer to shop at indie shops and local boutiques rather than chain stores. Most shops open around 10am, and close at 7pm. On weekends, though, they're generally open for a few hours from noon. Single-use plastic bags are banned in greener-than-green San Francisco, so bring a tote or expect to pay 25 cents for a paper bag.

ARTS & CULTURE

Sadly, culture isn't made available for everyone in San Francisco, with many museums charging a $25 entry fee. A solution: the CityPASS gives you up to 50 percent off entry to major attractions, though many of these still require a reservation. Theater tickets are similarly pricey, costing around $60, but you can find deals online. The dress code is the same throughout SF: jeans and sneakers all the way.

www.citypass.com

NIGHTLIFE

Nights out often start in a dive bar, with – as always – a low-key dress code. It's not unusual for clubbers to drive to and from their destination, especially young San Franciscans who are all about living healthily and drinking less. Locals don't pull all-nighters, especially as licensing laws mean most clubs close by 3am. Comedy clubs usually enforce a two-drink minimum. Whatever a night out entails, carding is rampant so ID is a must.

OUTDOORS

San Franciscans are an outdoorsy bunch and take good care of their city; littering carries a fine of $100. The city's few sandy strips are windy, so sunbathing isn't really the done thing. Karl, residents' nickname for the city's famous fog, can appear and disappear at any given moment, so always carry extra layers.

Keep in mind

Here are some more tips and tidbits that will help you fit in like a local.

» **Contactless** The majority of places take cards and use tap-to-pay tech like Square.

» **No smoking** Lighting up in public parks, plazas, and on state beaches is banned. Recreational cannabis is legal, though it's illegal to smoke it in the street.

» **Tipping** Tipping is expected by waitstaff and bartenders (per drink) and anything below 18 percent is considered a snub.

» **Stay hydrated** There are lots of water bottle refilling stations, so bring a reusable bottle.

GETTING AROUND

Occupying the peninsula between San Francisco Bay and the Pacific Ocean, San Francisco is a pretty small city – it measures just 7 miles by 7 miles (11 km by 11 km), and is home to fewer than a million people. It's divided into neighborhoods and "micro-hoods," some of which comprise only a handful of blocks. The city is built on 43 hills (the most famous are the Twin Peaks), hence its famously steep roads. A strict one-way system keeps those navigating these roads safe, and the city's simple grid pattern makes it easy to find your way around – though there is the odd hidden lane or crooked thoroughfare to throw you a curveball.

To keep things simple we've provided what3words addresses for each sight in this book, meaning you can quickly pinpoint exactly where you're heading.

On foot

Compact and gridded, San Francisco is entirely walkable. Downtown and the Mission, in particular, are forgivingly flat, while Nob Hill and Russian Hill reward steep climbs with spectacular views. Walking distances get a little more arduous once you're out on the avenues of the Richmond and Sunset but – wherever you're walking – you can enjoy the scenery and get a feel for each neighborhood. Sidewalks can get pretty busy with San Franciscans going about their buisness so try not to dawdle. If you do need to stop and check a what3words location, step to the inside of the sidewalk.

On wheels

Cycling is a great way to get around the city and soak up the scenery while pedaling. Alongside electric scooters and skateboards, the popularity of cycling is growing and the city's infrastructure is constantly being improved, with a network of bike lanes and routes regularly added. That said, super-hilly areas are best explored on foot. Cyclists should generally follow all the rules of the road, such as obeying traffic signals, signaling when turning, and giving way to pedestrians. California law requires cyclists to use reflectors and a front white light when riding. If using headphones, keep one ear free. And always wear a helmet. No arguments.

San Francisco doesn't have a comprehensive bikeshare scheme but Bay Wheels by Lyft allows you to rent bikes and ebikes from docking stations in the east of the city. A single ride costs $3 and a one-day pass costs just $10. *www.lyft.com*

By public transportation

The city has a range of public transportation options run by the San Francisco Municipal Transportation Agency (SFMTA): the Muni Metro light-rail, vintage F-line electric street trams, BART trains, and, of course, those iconic cable cars. Infuriatingly, however, few of these join up, and a lot of neighborhoods are served only by bus.

If you do take public transportation, make life easy and get a pre-loadable Clipper card to tap in and out of journeys. It works on everything, including cable cars and ferries. When taking the train, do as the locals do and line up politely at marked areas on the platform – don't just push your way on. A note on cable cars: lines to board are prohibitively long year-round, so either get an early start, or prepare to stand in line for an hour.

By car or taxi

Unless you have your own garage, parking is a nightmare in the city, made doubly fraught by frequent break-ins. Nightly hotel parking fees are high, too, so do yourself a favor and use Uber or Lyft if you need to take a car somewhere (only tourists use city cabs). Car rental is relatively cheap if you're looking to leave for a nearby escape *(p184)*; search for deals on Kayak or Getaround.

Download these

We recommend you download these apps to help you get about the city.

WHAT3WORDS
Your geocoding friend

A what3words address is a simple way to communicate any precise location on earth, using just three words. ///turns.desk.patio, for example, is the code for the Beat Museum entrance. Simply download the free what3words app, type a what3words address into the search bar, and you'll know exactly where to go.

TRANSIT
Your local transit advice

San Francisco mightn't have a cohesive public transportation system, but it does have a cohesive public transportation app. Transit predicts all bus and train arrivals, and calculates time and cost comparisons between Lyft's rideshares and bikeshares (provided there are Bay Wheels docks in your area).

San Francisco is a patchwork of mini-neighborhoods, each with its own distinct look and personality. Here we look at some of our favorites.

San Francisco
NEIGHBORHOODS

Bernal Heights

Liberals have long been attracted to this hilltop 'hood, which was a hotbed of activism in the 1980s. Bernal Heights is more domestic these days, with a lesbian community and cohort of young families earning the suburb the nickname "Maternal Heights." {map 4}

The Castro

An epicenter of the fight for LGBTQ+ rights in America since the 70s, the Castro is a queer utopia (think friendly locals, rainbow crosswalks, and gay bars galore). {map 2}

Chinatown

The nation's oldest Chinatown blends SF's Chinese community, old and new: from ornate temples and age-old fortune-cookie factories to sexy cocktail bars and airy art galleries. {map 1}

Cow Hollow

Yoga mamas and their strollers rule the sidewalks in Cow Hollow, where bougie fitness studios bump up against fancy restaurants and spenny boutiques. {map 5}

Dogpatch

Once a center of industry, Dogpatch is now the heartland of coffee-clutching creatives. Weekends are spent traipsing around the neighborhood's uber-cool art galleries and lusting after its warehouse loft apartments. {map 3}

The Embarcadero

Visitors flock to the waterfront Embarcadero to explore Pier 39 and Fisherman's Wharf. San Franciscans prefer to exercise along the boulevard before picking up treats from the Ferry Building. {map 1}

Haight-Ashbury

When young people met here to make love (not war) in 1967, Haight-Ashbury was anointed a hippie mecca. Years after the Summer of Love, laid-back locals still dig this groovy area for its casual brewpubs. {map 2}

Hayes Valley

Ditching its super-seedy rep, Hayes Valley is on the up. Its aspirational mix of Victorian townhouses and influx of top-notch dining spots and posh shopping options has tempted young monied professionals to put down roots here. {map 2}

Marina District

Imagine all the rich party kids from college moved to the same waterfront neighborhood; welcome to the Marina District. Yuppies live it up in the area's slick bars and restaurants before they settle down and start families in Cow Hollow. {map 5}

The Mission

Historically Latino, the city's hippest area is a colorful commotion of protest art, palm trees, and trendsetting food and drink spots. Sadly, since the dot-com boom of the 90s, gentrification has cast a shadow over the area, forcing many residents to move elsewhere. {map 4}

Nob Hill

Okay, the nickname "Snob Hill" might not paint this patch in the best light, but there's little doubt it's freakin' gorgeous. Old-money San

Francisco lords it over the rest of the city from Nob Hill, where cable cars rumble up steep streets with dazzling bay views. {map 1}

North Beach

Neighborhoods don't get more charming than North Beach. This old-school area is a lovely blend of Italian sidewalk cafés, revolutionary bookshops, and Beat-era saloons. {map 1}

Pacific Heights

Only celebrities and tech CEOs can afford to live in the mansions of SF's most expensive ocean-view neighborhood. But we can look (and dream). {map 5}

The Richmond

The residential avenues of Richmond border Golden Gate Park and stretch to Ocean Beach. Here a diverse mix of locals have transformed this outpost into a foodie Shangri-La. {map 5}

SOMA

SOMA stands for "South of the Market" and scoops up the area – wait for it – south

of Market Street. Start-up workers flock to the new-builds of this Downtown site, where warehouse nightclubs and trendy restaurants sit uncomfortably alongside homeless encampments. {map 3}

The Sunset

Perennially described as "Surfie," the Sunset district is certainly chilled-out, but don't expect sultry LA vibes: proximity to Ocean Beach makes it the foggiest area in town. {map 5}

Telegraph Hill

A picturesque oasis of bohemian cottages, preposterous gradients, and cascading cliffside gardens, this quiet residential spot offers superlatively scenic views – and feral parrots. No, seriously. {map 1}

Tenderloin

Blighted by homelessness and open drug use, this is notoriously the city's grittiest neighborhood but also one of the most creative, with a recent influx of art galleries and cocktail bars. {map 1}

San Francisco

ON THE MAP

Whether you're looking for your new favorite spot or want to check out what each part of San Francisco has to offer, our maps – along with handy map references throughout the book – have you covered.

Golden Gate
National
Recreation Area

Rodeo
Beach

P a c i f i c
O c e a n

0 kilometers   3

0 miles   3

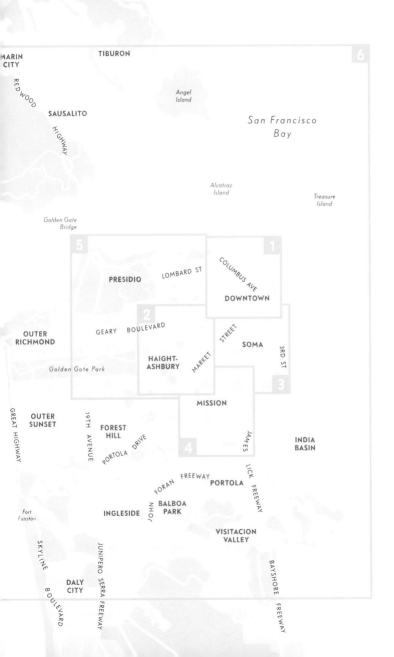

0 meters 500
0 yards 500

San Francisco
Bay

🅐 Musée Méchanique

THE EMBARCADERO

BEACH STREET

🅓 Buena Vista Cafe

BAY STREET

THE EMBARCADERO

BAY STREET

STOCKTON ST

HYDE STREET

LOMBARD ST

STREET

TELEGRAPH HILL

🅞 Greenwich Stairs

Cobb's Comedy Club 🅝 COLUMBUS

🅞 Filbert Street Stairs

🅔 The Italian Homemade Company

TAYLOR STREET

WASHINGTON SQUARE

NORTH BEACH

BATTERY ST

🅐 Exploratorium

RUSSIAN HILL

AVENUE

UNION STREET

🅓 Union Larder

STREET

Language of the Birds 🅐 🅐 The Beat Museum

BROADWAY

City Lights Booksellers 🅢
& Publishers

🅓 Comstock Saloon

BROADWAY

🅔 House of Nanking

WASHINGTON ST

🅢 Molte Cose
& Belle Cose

STOCKTON

LiPo Cocktail 🅓
Lounge

MARITIM PLAZA

Punch 🅝
Line

VAN

San Francisco
Cable Car Museum 🅐

CHINATOWN

MONTGOMERY

Embarcadero
Center Steps 🅒

🅢 ReLove WASHINGTON ST

NESS

🅓 Amelie

Chinese Historical Society 🅐
of America Museum

NOB HILL

Et Al. 🅐

🅔

FINANCIAL DISTRICT

STREET

Mister Jiu's

🅐 Good Vibrations Grace Cathedral 🅐

AVENUE

Tonga Room 🅓
& Hurricane Bar

CALIFORNIA ST

ST. MARYS SQUARE

MARKET

Contraband 🅓
Coffee Bar CALIFORNIA ST

SF Masonic 🅐

🅓

STREET

Out of 🅢
the Closet

Top of the Mark

BUSH STREET

Best of
San Francisco
Stand-Up Comedy 🅝

The Flying Falafel 🅔

Pacific Cocktail Haven 🅓 Cheaper Than

BUSH STREET

Secret Improv Society 🅝🅝 Therapy

🅔 Rooster & Rice

🅐 San Francisco Playhouse

2ND STREET

HYDE STREET

620 Jones
🅓

TAYLOR STREET

UNION SQUARE

Bini's Kitchen 🅔

Jay Jeffers – 🅢
The Studio

Resolute 🅓

Curran 🅐🅐 American
Conservatory Theater

3RD STREET

STREET

GEARY STREET

Bourbon & 🅓
Branch

THEATER DISTRICT

MARKET STREET

STREET

4TH STREET

SOMA

TENDERLOIN

STREET

MAP 1

Blue Bottle
Coffee 🅓
    🅔 Humphry
    Slocombe

STREET

Angler 🅔

Rincon Center 🅐
    Murals

BEALE

STREET

Rooftop
Tai Chi

ST

STREET

MAP 2

2

GOUGH STREET

Jefferson
Square

Smuggler's
Cove D

FULTON STREET

GOUGH STREET

Marine
Layer S   Nightbird
               E

STREET

Rich Table E

Zuni Cafe E

STREET

MARKET
        S
        Grooves
        Inspiralled Vinyl

16TH STREET

VALENCIA

MISSION
DOLORES

DOLORES STREET

STREET

STREET

E EAT

Miyako's Old-Fashioned
  Ice Cream Shop *(p38)*
Nari *(p49)*
Nightbird *(p43)*
Rich Table *(p40)*
State Bird Provisions *(p45)*
The Progress *(p41)*
Zuni Cafe *(p33)*

D DRINK

Magnolia Brewing *(p72)*
Last Rites *(p63)*
Twin Peaks Tavern *(p66)*
Smuggler's Cove *(p61)*

S SHOP

Amoeba Music *(p93)*
Booksmith *(p103)*
Bound Together Anarchist
  Collective Bookstore *(p101)*
Grooves Inspiralled Vinyl *(p93)*
Kenneth Wingard *(p97)*
Local Take *(p88)*
Marine Layer *(p89)*
Originals Vinyl *(p94)*
Relic Vintage *(p107)*
Rooky Ricardo's Records *(p92)*
Vinyl Dreams *(p95)*
The Wasteland *(p107)*

A ARTS & CULTURE

African American Art & Culture
  Complex *(p129)*
GLBT Historical Society
  Museum *(p112)*
Haight-Ashbury Clock *(p116)*
Lorraine Hansberry Theater *(p127)*
Rainbow Honor Walk *(p118)*

N NIGHTLIFE

Beaux *(p156)*
Boom Boom Room *(p136)*
Castro Theatre *(p149)*
The Fillmore *(p137)*
Hi Tops *(p159)*
The Independent *(p136)*
Lookout *(p159)*
Madrone Art Bar *(p140)*
The Mix *(p157)*
New People Cinema *(p151)*
Open Mic at Cafe International
  (p154)
Poetry at the Sacred Grounds *(p152)*
Sheba Piano Lounge *(p139)*

O OUTDOORS

The Castro to Twin Peaks *(p183)*
Corona Heights Park *(p165)*
Mission Dolores Park *(p164)*
Vulcan Steps *(p170)*

MAP 3

3

21st Amendment
Brewery & Restaurant
D

Sailing Trips **O**
Kayaking Tours **O**
HINA
ASIN   Sea Change
            Kinetic Sculpture **A**

3RD
STREET

MISSION
BAY

16TH STREET
STEM Kitchen **E**
& Garden

DOGPATCH

3RD
STREET

FREEWAY

E EAT

Benu (p50)
Brenda's French Soul Food (p35)
In Situ (p45)
Kin Khao (p44)
Niku Steakhouse (p47)
Rintaro (p51)
STEM Kitchen & Garden (p43)

D DRINK

21st Amendment Brewery &
    Restaurant (p73)
Anchor Public Taps (p74)
B Restaurant & Bar (p79)
Black Hammer Brewing (p74)
Charmaine's Rooftop
    Bar & Lounge (p76)
Dirty Habit (p76)
Press Club (p68)
Sightglass Coffee (p82)
Terroir (p71)
Whitechapel (p63)

S SHOP

BaBoo (p98)
McGuire Furniture (p99)
Zozi's Loft (p99)

A ARTS & CULTURE

Catharine Clark Gallery (p130)
Luggage Store Gallery (p130)
Museum of the African
    Diaspora (p115)

New Conservatory Theatre
    Center (p126)
Sea Change Kinetic Sculpture (p121)
SOMArts Cultural Center (p128)
SFMOMA (p112)
Tenderloin Museum (p119)

N NIGHTLIFE

AMC Metreon 16 (p149)
Asia SF (p155)
Audio (p142)
Black Cat (p137)
Bawdy Storytelling (p154)
Butter (p142)
Cat Club (p140)
The EndUp (p143)
Great American Music Hall (p139)
Moad Open Mic (p154)
Mortified Live (p152)
OASIS (p159)
PianoFight (p146)
Raven Bar (p143)
Rickshaw Stop (p136)
The Setup (p147)
SF Eagle (p157)
Temple (p141)

O OUTDOORS

Kayaking Tours (p172)
Sailing Trips (p173)

MAP 4

POTRERO

STREET

5TH

AVENUE

JAMES LICK FREEWAY

POTRERO

AVENUE

JAMES LICK FREEWAY

 Barebottle Brewing

San Francisco Bay

0 meters 800
0 yards 800

Crissy Field

MARINA BOULEVARD

FILLMORE STREET

BOULEVARD

LINCOLN

PRESIDIO PARKWAY

Oceanic Society Whale Watching ⊙

MARINA

California Wine Merchant Ⓓ
LOMBAR

DIVISADERO STREET

Atelier Ⓔ Crenn

Baker Beach ⊙ Sand Ladder
The Presidio ⊙

Baker Beach

⊙ Batteries to Bluffs Trail

PRESIDIO

Lyon Street Steps ⊙
Lyon Street Steps to ⊙ Palace of Fine Arts

Alta Plaza Park ⊙

Sunset Yoga ⊙

LINCOLN BOULEVARD

Bay Area Ridge Trail ⊙ Ⓐ

Andy Goldsworthy Sculptures

PRESIDIO HEIGHTS

⊙

Sunrise H Workout

March Ⓢ

The Great Cable Car Chase ⊙

STREET

CALIFORNIA

PARK PRESIDIO BOULEVARD

STREET

Green Apple Books Ⓢ

CALIFORNIA

Ⓔ Pizzetta 211

Ⓔ B Star Bar

BOULEVARD

DIVISADERO STREET

Breadbelly Ⓔ

RICHMOND

GEARY BOULEVARD

INNER RICHMOND

8TH AVENUE

High Treason Ⓓ

ARGUELLO BLVD

STANYAN STREET

GEARY BOULEVARD

St. John Coltrane Ⓐ Church

19TH AVENUE

FULTON STREET

STANYAN STREET

FULTON STREET

FELL STREET
OAK STREET

Panhandle

HAIGHT-ASHBURY

Buena Vista Park

Golden Gate Park ⊙

California Academy Ⓐ of Sciences

Zumba in ⊙ the Park

Corona Heights Park

LINCOLN WAY

19TH AVENUE

Inner Sunset Flea Ⓢ

7TH AVENUE

STANYAN STREET

JUDAH STREET

INNER SUNSET

Mount Sutro

17TH STREET
MARKET STREET

Hidden Garden Stairs ⊙

Tank Hill ⊙ Park

MAP 5

E EAT

D DRINK

S SHOP

A ARTS & CULTURE

O OUTDOORS

0 kilometers 2
0 miles 2

TIBURON

Sea Trek Stand Up
Paddleboard Center

Angel Island
Immigration Station

Angel
Island

SAUSALITO

REDWOOD

Golden Gate National
Recreation Area

HIGHWAY

San Francisco
Bay

Alcatraz
Island

Rodeo
Beach

Golden Gate
Bridge

LOMBARD ST

COLUMBUS AVE

MARKET ST

GEARY BOULEVARD

See maps 1–5 for
Central San Francisco

Land's End to
Baker Beach

OUTER
RICHMOND

MARKET ST

SOUTH VAN NESS AVE

Balboa Theater N S Noise
N

Purusha in the Park

Saturday Night at
La Promenade Cafe

General Store S S Black Bird
Trouble Coffee Company D E Bookstore
Outerlands

Andytown Coffee Roasters D

OUTER
SUNSET

GREAT HIGHWAY

19TH AVENUE

16th Avenue
Tiled Steps

FOREST
HILL

PORTOLA DRIVE

Glen Canyon
Park

JAMES

Pacific
Ocean

Mount
Davidson

Alemany S
Flea Market

PORTOLA

LICK FREEWAY

Fort
Funston

JOHN FORAN FREEWAY

INGLESIDE

BALBOA
PARK

VISITACION
VALLEY

Surfing Lessons
8 miles (13 km)

DALY CITY

MAP 6

Treasure Island

Kite The Bay

Mad Oak
7 miles (11 km)

3RD STREET

E Besharam

INDIA
BASIN

E EAT

Besharam *(p54)*
Outerlands *(p32)*

D DRINK

Andytown Coffee Roasters *(p81)*
Mad Oak *(p79)*
Trouble Coffee Company *(p80)*

S SHOP

Alemany Flea Market *(p105)*
Black Bird Bookstore *(p103)*
General Store *(p96)*
Noise *(p92)*

A ARTS & CULTURE

Angel Island Immigration Station
(p118)

N NIGHTLIFE

Balboa Theater *(p148)*
Saturday Night at La Promenade
Cafe *(p155)*

O OUTDOORS

16th Avenue Tiled Steps *(p169)*
Glen Canyon Park *(p166)*
Kite the Bay *(p172)*
Lands End to Baker Beach *(p180)*
Mount Davidson *(p183)*
Purusha in the Park *(p179)*
Sea Trek Stand Up Paddleboard
Center *(p175)*
Surfing Lessons *(p173)*

EAT

San Franciscans love to get creative with food. Chefs blend cuisines to make new flavors, and restaurants celebrate ingredients in season. The result? An ever-evolving food scene.

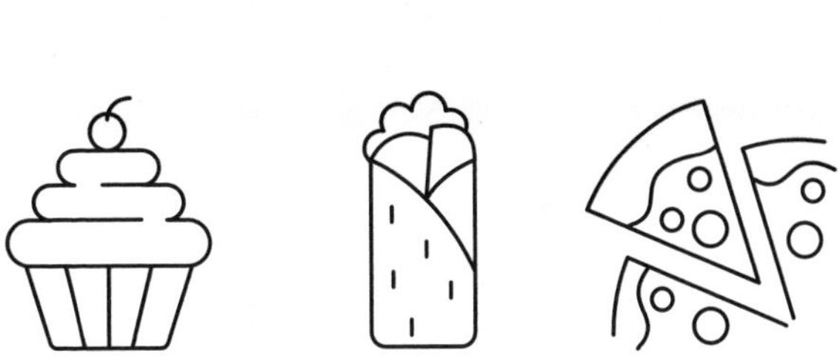

Brunch Spots

Trust San Francisco to give brunch – the all-American meal – its own signature spin. Jump out of bed for farm-fresh staples and imaginative dishes that draw inspiration from the city's proud immigrant cultures.

OUTERLANDS

Map 6; 4001 Judah Street, Outer Sunset; ///commented.lime.fakes; www.outerlandssf.com

It's testament to the food at Outerlands that you can bet on a wait, in spite of its not-exactly-coveted location in the outer reaches of SF's notoriously foggy Sunset district. Surfers are regulars here, coming back time after time for the kitchen's twists on breakfast classics, like the egg baked into a doorstop-sized slice of Outerlands' famous levain bread and served with braised farm greens and Calabrian chili.

B STAR BAR

Map 5; 127 Clement Street, Inner Richmond; ///foster.means.intent; www.bstarbar.com

Star by name, star by nature. While countless hungry locals get up early to join the line at Burma Superstar, those in-the-know instead head to sister café B Star Bar, which is just one block away. It almost always has spare seats and serves up a well-priced weekend brunch that runs the gamut from French toast to Pan-Asian bowls. Be sure to extend a sympathetic nod to the hungry hordes waiting for Burma Superstar as you leave.

FOREIGN CINEMA

**Map 4; 2534 Mission Street, The Mission; ///object.inner.woods;
www.foreigncinema.com**

Probably the city's most enduringly popular brunch spot, the Mission's Foreign Cinema lacks for nothing. Cool setting? Check: it's a former movie theater. Hip SF twists on breakfast items? You got it: how about an organic "Pop Tart," with fillings like wild huckleberry or pineapple, Dungeness crab frittatas, or Monterey Bay calamari?

» Don't leave without impressing your brunch date with a visit to Modernism West, an art gallery accessed via Foreign Cinema's patio.

ZUNI CAFE

**Map 2; 1658 Market Street, Hayes Valley; ///bands.upset.loaf;
www.zunicafe.com**

It can be hard amid all the hipsterness to find a slice of old-school San Francisco – which is where this local institution, a firm favorite since 1979, comes in. Zuni Cafe is at once typically laid-back and extra special. Bow-tie-clad barmen shake classic cocktails, a piano player tinkles, and dressed-down diners happily wait an hour for the famous wood-fired roast chicken. All of this combined makes Zuni Cafe a great spot to bring the parents.

Solo, Pair, Crowd

After a table for one? Or in search of a family-style feast? San Francisco has the perfect brunch spot for you.

FLYING SOLO

Banter at the bar

Single diners score a spot fast at Swan Oyster Depot in Polk Gulch, a 108-year-old, 18-seat raw bar with the freshest local seafood and super-chatty staff.

IN A PAIR

Catch-ups and cable cars

Grab a sidewalk table for two outside Nob Hill's Mymy and gossip over eggs Benedict and banana-soufflé pancakes as cable cars rumble by.

FOR A CROWD

Dumplings by the dozen

The dim sum menu at Inner Richmond's beloved Dragon Beaux restaurant is absolutely enormous: you'll need a crew to do it justice. Don't miss the multicolored "Five Guys Xiao Long Bao" dumplings.

BRENDA'S FRENCH SOUL FOOD

Map 3; 652 Polk Street, Tenderloin; ///leans.busy.dollar;
www.frenchsoulfood.com

Chalk your name on Brenda's blackboard for a table because, boy,
is the Cali-Creole comfort food worth the wait. Here, Louisiana
classics like buttery biscuits and cheddar grits share a plate with SF
originals, such as "hangtown fry" (a crispy oyster and bacon omelet).
» **Don't leave without** trying a crawfish beignet, a sort-of-savory,
cayenne-dusted donut stuffed with crawfish, scallions, and cheese.

JANE ON FILLMORE

Map 5; 2123 Fillmore Street, Pacific Heights; ///tune.form.appeal;
www.itsjane.com

Lycra-clad yogis might lean toward the granola and smoothie
bowls here but, for us, it's all about Jane's aspirational toast menu.
That's right, even toast has gone gourmet in San Francisco, with
everything from Danish rye to gluten-free quinoa loaves, all of
which are topped with delicious seasonal offerings.

GRACIAS MADRE

Map 4; 2211 Mission Street, The Mission; ///common.clots.stones;
www.gracias-madre.com

From the looks of it, every vegan in the Bay Area comes here on the
weekend. Why? This Mexican restaurant gives the vegan treatment
to American fare like sausage and potato hash (it's tempeh chorizo)
and French toast (topped with cashew cream). Delicious.

Bakeries and Ice Cream Parlors

San Franciscans take their sweet tooth seriously: residents routinely line up for cult pastries or boutique ice-cream scoops crafted with regional ingredients. Vegan options are, naturally, standard.

TARTINE BAKERY

Map 4; 600 Guerrero Street, The Mission; ///coffee.diary.museum; www.tartinebakery.com

Tartine is a bit like San Francisco: small and unassuming, yet super-influential. Take the morning bun, a sticky, orange-and-cinnamon phenomenon that locals rightly rave about. The bakery also does a great bread pudding, which friends share at the smattering of tables.

ETERNA PRIMAVERA

Map 4; 2951 24th Street, The Mission; ///bother.create.when; 415-932-6295

This no-frills *panaderia* (bakery) is a staple in the Latin American community and has survived years of displacement (thank rising rents). Owner Manuel Barrientos learned the art of baking traditional

Mexican *pan dulce* (sweet breads) and Guatemalan pastries from his father, a first-generation immigrant who started his own bakery in the neighborhood decades before. For a taste of the Mission's roots, pull up a chair, grab a cinnamon-flecked pastry, and, if you know your Spanish, keep an ear out for local gossip.

SALT & STRAW

Map 5; 2201 Fillmore Street, Pacific Heights; ///range.rift.natively; www.saltandstraw.com

Okay, you might have to join a line under the candy-striped awning at this place. But it moves fast, and you won't find flavors like this anyplace else. Literally: the West Coast mini-chain churns flavors specific to each city, usng hyperlocal purveyors. Here in SF it's all about the Mount Tam ice cream (hello candied chunks of walnut levain).

CRAFTSMAN AND WOLVES

Map 4; 746 Valencia Street, The Mission; ///cheeks.wonderfully.flags; www.craftsman-wolves.com

Locals love this industrial-chic patisserie in the Mission because they never know what it's going to do next. The display case by the cash register is a museum-quality exhibit of sugary works of art. That over-sized, bright-yellow pill capsule? That is in fact honey-infused mousse and honey chamomile curd on beeswax walnut shortbread. Well, sure, what else?

» Don't leave without trying the raspberry chocolate travel cake – you'd never guess it was vegan and gluten-free.

HUMPHRY SLOCOMBE

Map 1; Ferry Building, Embarcadero; ///water.fires.sculpture;
www.humphryslocombe.com

This creamery scoops wildly original flavors, with cones filled with everything from mushroom to prosciutto. Most popular among patrons – granddads and young-guns alike – is the "Secret Breakfast": bourbon ice-cream flecked with caramelized cornflakes.

BREADBELLY

Map 5; 1408 Clement Street, Inner Richmond; ///lanes.oven.comet;
www.breadbellysf.com

The next-gen Asian-American treats here are as luminous as this bakery's teal-painted front. Signature slices of vivid-green "kaya toast" – Japanese milk bread smothered in Malaysian pandan and coconut curd – fast amassed a dedicated fan following.

» Don't leave without sampling the neighborhood favorites: the purple roasted potato meringue tart and toasted pecan and red bean buns.

MIYAKO'S OLD-FASHIONED ICE CREAM SHOP

Map 2; 1470 Fillmore Street, Fillmore; ///lows.drop.deeper; 415-931-5260

This sweet little shop's chaotic interior, with all manner of handwritten signs and sweet-jar-lined shelves, is wonderfully nostalgic and long-time owner Thomas Bennett knows all his many regulars by name. It's also one of the last remaining Black-owned businesses in Fillmore, a neighborhood once known as "the Harlem of the West."

Liked by the locals

"When one of our store's windows was broken, people poured in to support us in getting it fixed. I'll forever be grateful for how people in this city come together for each other."

THOMAS BENNETT, OWNER OF MIYAKO'S
OLD-FASHIONED ICE CREAM SHOP

Farm-to-Table

Farm-to-table isn't a buzzphrase in San Francisco: it's an out-and-out obsession. With countless organic producers surrounding the city, many ingredients take just hours to journey from pasture to plate.

RICH TABLE

Map 2; 199 Gough Street, Hayes Valley; ///quiet.extra.occupy; www.richtablesf.com

This husband-and-wife-run neighborhood stalwart could hardly be more San Franciscan. From the spare, salvaged wood interiors to the deceptively simple menu, it's everything locals love in a restaurant. Here an ordinary-sounding "sardine chip" is actually a potato chip with a sardine fillet weaved into it, while the simple donut is made with porcini and dunked in raclette.

AL'S PLACE

Map 4; 1499 Valencia Street, The Mission; ///newest.split.bonds; www.alsplacesf.com

Chef Aaron London based his menu around a unique concept: veggie entrées accompanied by optional meat and seafood sides. And these aren't just any greens; they're the spoils of Blue Dane

Garden, a biodynamic Californian farm. This, married with London's attentive cooking (he spends days pickling and brining), quickly won fans, and nabbing a reservation is still tough.

» **Don't leave without** ordering the French fries: brined for 96 hours, fried for six minutes, and served with smoked-apple barbecue sauce.

PIZZETTA 211
Map 5; 211 23rd Avenue, Outer Richmond; ///youth.desks.soda; www.pizzetta211.com

It'd be easy to miss this tiny gem, were it not for the line of hopefuls hovering on the sidewalk, peering into the display windows and praying for a seat. They come for San Francisco's best pizza, made to order in the Lilliputian open kitchen, and topped with seasonal ingredients like local corn, farm eggs, and white anchovies (the menu changes every other week). Weekday lunchtimes are best for scoring a table.

THE PROGRESS
Map 2; 1525 Fillmore Street, Hayes Valley; ///feels.brick.cups; www.statebirdsf.com

Stuart Brioza and Nicole Krasinski became local celebs after opening their first restaurant, the much-lauded State Bird Provisions *(p45)*, and their second restaurant, The Progress, doesn't disappoint. You won't find many solo diners or dates here – a group is needed to tackle the onslaught of seasonal small plates. We're talking wasabi-lime beets and grilled octopus, with toasted black rice and preserved lemon.

Liked by the locals

"The Bay Area food world is special because of its access to agriculture. The amazing farms entice the best chefs, who then open up unique restaurants that change the whole country's view on food."

KIM ALTER, CHEF AT NIGHTBIRD

STEM KITCHEN AND GARDEN

Map 3; 499 Illinois Street, The Mission; ///took.gentle.pitch;
www.stemkitchensf.com

One of the best rooftop dining spaces in San Francisco, this modern restaurant's unpretentious decor is matched by its straightforward organic cuisine – think build-your-own salads, sandwiches, and pizzas. For a spot of after-dinner fun, strike up a game of bocce, perhaps while nursing one of the seasonal garden shrub sodas.

NIGHTBIRD

Map 2; 330 Gough Street, Hayes Valley; ///into.scan.fade;
www.nightbirdrestaurant.com

Behind a solid wood door carved with an owl, chef Kim Alter's minimalist bistro has been quietly blowing Hayes Valley minds with its artistic, produce-forward "five course and five bite" set menus. Note, the utterly delicious vegetarian menu costs $45 less than the meat.
» Don't leave without trying a tipple at the Linden Room, Alter's adjoining cocktail bar, where seasonal fruits and herbs are used.

WILDSEED

Map 5; 2000 Union Street, Cow Hollow; ///rider.alert.fields;
www.wildseedsf.com

Seasonal eating is about sustainability as much as flavor, and nowhere is this more ingrained than at this vegan restaurant in bougie Cow Hollow. Here, San Francisco's beautiful and super-healthy feast on beetroot poke and asparagus-studded pasta.

Special Occasion

San Francisco is a casual town, and that extends to its most upscale restaurants. Even so, it's easy to find the gravitas and glamour that birthdays, engagements, and promotions demand.

KIN KHAO

Map 3; 55 Cyril Magnin Street, Tenderloin; ///often.blame.juror; www.kinkhao.com

Don't judge this hotel restaurant by its admittedly dull cover. Chef Pim Techamuanvivit has made Kin Khao an unlikely must-dine spot by the sheer force of her fiery cooking, whipping up fresh curry pastes memorized from her childhood in Thailand, and blending them with a San Franciscan sensibility (think Dungeness crab noodles).

LAZY BEAR

Map 4; 3416 19th Street, The Mission; ///slower.drew.minus; www.lazybearsf.com

San Franciscan foodies come again and again to this buzzy "dinner-party restaurant." Guests begin their evening with cocktails and canapés in the "Den," before sitting down together at two extra-long tables. Chefs take turns to tell the story of each dish

Tickets to Lazy Bear are released a month in advance, on the 15th of each month. Sign up to the newsletter to get a reminder.

between courses, and even invite diners into the open kitchen. The ever-changing, multicourse menu of hyper-seasonal fare is well worth the ticket fee, but meeting new foodie friends? Priceless.

IN SITU

Map 3; 151 3rd Street, SoMa; ///softly.polite.tigers; insitu.sfmoma.org

On the first floor of SFMOMA, In Situ acts as a sort of rotating exhibition of the world's greatest epicurean artists, with the kitchen reproducing dishes from famous restaurants including Copenhagen's Noma, New York City's Eleven Madison Park, and Barcelona's Tickets. The set lunch menu is a steal at three courses for $45.

STATE BIRD PROVISIONS

Map 2; 1529 Fillmore Street, Fillmore; ///nature.closed.glad; www.statebirdsf.com

There is no menu at State Bird Provisions. Instead, waitstaff bring around carts and trays of various imaginative, regionally sourced small plates, from which you'll pick whatever catches your eye. It makes for a gloriously social and surprising evening, where you're never quite sure what your next bite will be – well, apart from outstandingly good. Reservations are impossible, but line up outside at 5pm and you should snag the first seating (doors open 5:30pm).

» Don't leave without sharing the burrata-topped, deep-fried garlic bread – it's a mainstay on the nightly changing menu for good reason.

BLUE PLATE

Map 4; 3218 Mission Street, Bernal Heights; ///loans.cabin.laptop; www.blueplatesf.com

Right where the happening Mission district meets sleepier Bernal Heights, this blue-brick mainstay is where the city's top chefs head for a taste of fresh California fare, without the sky-high price. Industry insiders love how the region's finest produce is used to comforting, unfussy effect, like chicken wings smothered in local Point Reyes blue cheese. If it's warm, ask for a table in the cute garden out back.

ATELIER CRENN

Map 5; 3127 Fillmore Street, Cow Hollow; ///passes.salt.unable; www.ateliercrenn.com

Any local foodie worth their Himalayan salt has saved up to dine at SF's most expensive restaurant (you have been warned). They say it's worth it, because there's nothing typical about Atelier Crenn.

China Live's Eight Tables *(www.chinalivesf.com)*, by chef George Chen, is the alpha and omega of hush-hush gastronomic outings in the city. Inspiration comes from the dining style Si Fang Cai – a.k.a. "Private Chateau Cuisine" – which hints at the intimate supper clubs of the Song Dynasty. Si Fang Cai is a personal experience, like you're eating in someone's home. And China Live's Eight Tables really achieves this.

Firstly, it's the nation's only three-Michelin-starred restaurant helmed by a female chef (Dominique Crenn). It's reassuringly unassuming, tucked between a chiropractor and a dry-cleaners. And the menu arrives in the form of a poem. It's utterly joyous.

NIKU STEAKHOUSE

Map 3; 61 Division Street, Financial District; ///risk.fault.exists; www.nikusteakhouse.com

Having suffered damage from a fire in 2020 – shortly after opening, no less – Niku Steakhouse has proven a resilient newcomer on the gastronomic block. One of SF's best stops for authentic Wagyu beef, the Financial District eatery is the perfect place to celebrate a life event. And if you really want to splash out, the one-of-a-kind Japanese whiskey room can be reserved for larger parties.

» Don't leave without ordering the dry-aged Wagyu beef and the raw, purple sea urchin uni, served atop authentic Japanese dishware.

ANGLER

Map 1; 132 The Embarcadero, Embarcadero; ///spoon.flows.aspect; www.anglerrestaurants.com

Angler was an instant hit among San Franciscans, largely thanks to chef Joshua Skenes. His signature technique – painstakingly cooking food over a wood-burning hearth – is here applied to seafood from the Pacific coast. But the difference between Angler and Skenes' other restaurant, city-stalwart Saison, is that instead of being restricted to a pricey ten-course menu, the menu is (semi-) affordably à-la-carte.

California Fusion

*Maybe the most authentic taste of the City by the Bay
is found in its fusion restaurants, where chefs'
ancestral dishes are suffused with the booty of Bay
Area farms. You won't find these eats anywhere else.*

KAIYŌ

Map 5; 1838 Union Street, Cow Hollow; ///froze.abode.bolts;
www.kaiyosf.com

Relative newcomer KAIYŌ has been making waves for its craft
cocktails and left-of-center take on Peruvian and Japanese cuisines.
Enjoy fresh ceviches paired with authentic Japanese Wagyu meats;
the bowled offerings (many of which are garnished with edible flowers)
are as pretty as they are delicious. Thirsty? Try a Peruvian pisco.

FLOUR + WATER

Map 4; 2401 Harrison Street, The Mission; ///clap.toward.choice;
www.flourandwater.com

It's notoriously SF's toughest reservation, but here's the good news:
Flour + Water holds 75 percent of its tables for walk-ins, so turn up at
opening and you'll be seated within the hour. Founder Thomas
McNaughton learned the art of obscure regional pastas from nonnas

Once your name's on the list here, wait it out across the street at Trick Dog – it's on the "World's 50 Best Bars" list every year.

in Bologna. Now, he dresses those next-level pastas in the Bay Area harvest's finest (from pickled kumquats to foraged black trumpets). Plus, the poppy playlist makes every meal here feel like a celebration.

LIHOLIHO YACHT CLUB

Map 4; 3560 18th Street, The Mission;
///count.flap.chill; www.liholihoyachtclub.com

From the potted palms to the color-splashed terrace, this "Caliwaii" restaurant is an instant breath of fresh, tropical air. Chef Ravi Kapur brings the flavors of his Honolulu-spent childhood (look out for pictures of his beloved mom) into ultramodern focus with snappy local flavors and Pan-Asian punches. This place is always a party, populated by good-time folk clinking cocktails and diving into shared dishes.

» Don't leave without ordering the Baked Hawaii, a remixed Baked Alaska with pineapple ice-cream and oh-so-perfectly scorched meringue.

NARI

Map 2; 1625 Post Street, Pacific Heights;
///shower.gent.tile; www.narisf.com

Chef and restaurateur Pim Techamuanvivit – of Kin Khao (p44) fame – brings you this modern, women-led eatery (the clue is in the name: "nari" comes from the Thai word for "women"), inspired by the women who taught her to cook. Expect punchy Thai flavors paired with Californian sensibility and ingredients.

BENU

Map 3; 22 Hawthorne Street, SoMa; ///fired.scary.reader
www.benusf.com

You might need the salary of a San Francisco techie to eat here, but what else would you expect from a consistent entry in the "World's 50 Best Restaurants"? Benu blends chef Corey Lee's Korean heritage with French cooking techniques and California ingredients: think foie gras xiao long bao or frog legs with mountain yam.

MISTER JIU'S

Map 1; 28 Waverley Place, Chinatown; ///legal.crew.tasty;
www.misterjius.com

The Cali-Cantonese menu here is full of clever nods to the city, and spotting them makes diners feel in on the secret. Scallion pancakes have the acid tang of sourdough, the bread San Francisco invented, while barbecue pork buns recall a Dutch crunch, yet another city bread sensation with a crackly, rice-flour top. Chef-owner Brandon Jew is an SF native who grew up eating at Chinatown banquets. His

Try it!
LEARN FROM THE BEST

Dined at Mister Jiu's and now a little obsessed with Cali-Cantonese cuisine? Make your own dishes with Brandon Jew, the chef-owner, at one of his cooking courses (www.sfcooking.com).

restaurant is an ode to the community old and new: weaving the traditional (check out the salvaged lotus chandeliers) with a modern energy (home-cured charcuterie and craft drinks).

RINTARO

Map 3; 82 14th Street, SoMa; ///fees.editor.jeeps;
www.izakayarintaro.com

Only those in-the-know could guess at what's behind the fence at 82 14th Street. The *izakaya* (gastropub) – filled with gourmands giddy at finding SF's finest Japanese food – looks like it dropped straight out of Kyoto. Owner Sylvan Mishima Brackett was born there, but raised in California, where he trained under the OG farm-to-table chef Alice Waters. At Rintaro, he blends the best of both worlds: see the Japanese fried chicken stuffed with Sonoma-churned cheese.

CALIFORNIOS

Map 4; 3115 22nd Street, The Mission;
www.californiossf.com;///loser.likely.afford

"Californios" are Hispanic people native to California; it's a term suited to this modern Mexican restaurant, run by a Mexican-Venezuelan chef in the Latin-flavored Mission district. Val M. Cantu blends the region's seasonal pickings with the cookery of his lineage, to Michelin-starred effect. The upshot is an incredibly personal menu that raises the neighborhood's street taco fare more than just a notch.

» Don't leave without savoring the "three beans," which supercharges the Mexican food staple to indulgent and delicious levels.

Cheap Eats

San Francisco isn't exactly synonymous with cheap ($16 sandwiches are as common as cable cars), but while its food-infatuated residents might be happy to forgo rent to eat, you can still dine out on a budget.

TAQUERIA CANCUN

Map 4; 2288 Mission Street, The Mission;
///spell.ground.fields; 415-252-9560

La Taqueria might have the longest line of the Mission's hole-in-the-wall eateries, but old-timers and tech bros alike know that the area's best cheap eats are found behind the red-and-yellow facade of Taqueria Cancun. Skip the hefty "Mission burritos" and go for the fresh-flavored tacos (al pastor and beef tongue are popular), slather it all in house salsa, and wash it down with a proper Mexican Coke.

ROOSTER & RICE

Map 1; 2211 Filbert Street, Cow Hollow; ///decide.timing.first;
www.roosterandrice.com

When not downward-dogging, Cow Hollow's yoga moms flock to this shoebox-sized counter spot for a fix of $12 *khao mun gai* – a pile of fragrant rice with steamed chicken, cucumber, and an insanely addictive chili, ginger, and garlic sauce. The only item on the menu, this Thai street-food favorite was made for on-the-go eating, which is lucky seeing as there are only three tiny tables out front.

PEACHES PATTIES

Map 4; 2948 Folsom Street, The Mission; ///pure.mobile.debit; www.peachespatties.com

When Shani Jones couldn't find Jamaican food in San Francisco outside of her mother's house, she decided to do something about it. With the help of La Cocina – a San Francisco nonprofit that empowers low-income women of color to launch food businesses – she's bringing her family's Jamaican patty recipes to the masses. These flaky, turmeric-spiked pastries come stuffed with ground beef, chicken curry, or lentils.

» Don't leave without sipping Shani's homemade, fresh ginger beer. No, it's not alcoholic and, yes, it's ultra-zingy and super-refreshing.

THE ITALIAN HOMEMADE COMPANY

Map 1; 716 Columbus Avenue, North Beach; ///flown.natively.minds; www.italianhomemade.com

Don't fret about the lack of tables in this counter-service Italian: the bargain pastas and *piadinas* (flatbread) are best enjoyed a block over, in Washington Square. Here, surrounded by Little Italy's sidewalk cafés, enjoy a picnic of stuffed flatbreads and saucy pastas, hand-made by a trio of cooks from Italy's gourmet Emilia-Romagna region. They've opened three additional locations – but the original is the best.

BESHARAM

Map 6; 1275 Minnesota Street, Dogpatch; ///losses.windy.enjoyable;
www.besharamrestaurant.com

At Besharam, chef Heena Patel serves up mostly vegetarian Gujurati
food, a regional cuisine that doesn't get much traction outside of
India. But it should: the squash dumplings and blue cheese *parathas*
dunked into tangy, sweet-and-sour chutneys are mouthwateringly
good. Early-bird dinners only; the kitchen closes at 7pm.

» Don't leave without sharing a slice of Patel's shrikhand cheesecake,
an American twist on the sweet, cardamom, and saffron-spiced curd.

THE FLYING FALAFEL

Map 1; 1051 Market Street, Mid-Market; ///camps.flat.views;
www.flyingfalafel.com

Join the line at this super-small vegan spot for low-cost pita pockets,
loaded with crispy falafel balls, veggies, pickles, and sesame or spicy
sauce. There's usually a bench on the sidewalk with a couple of
stools, but this is likely a to-go meal. Don't let that stop you ordering
the vegan cheesecake, though – we guarantee no buyer's remorse.

BINI'S KITCHEN

Map 1; McKesson Plaza, 1 Post Street, Financial District;
///single.quench.limit; www.biniskitchen.com

The Financial District generally deals in two types of fare: swanky
steakhouses for venture capitalists with expense accounts or grab-
and-go lunchtime chains catering to office workers eating "al desko."

But lo, opposite the Montgomery BART station there lies a beacon of hope. Suited bankers and skateboarding creatives alike make for Bini's bright kiosk at lunchtime for real-deal Nepalese *momos* and curries (chef Bini grew up in Kathmandu). Weekdays only; closes 3pm.

HOUSE OF NANKING

Map 1; 919 Kearny Street, Chinatown; ///rushed.timing.swept; www.houseofnanking.net

Eating at this no-frills Chinatown classic might involve getting cajoled by the serving staff, but there's a reason that residents, travelers, and celebrities alike all keep lining up: the food really is that good. The waiters will tell you, rather than ask you, what you're going to eat: sharing plates piled with sesame chicken atop sliced sweet potatoes, and off-menu items like lightly breaded jumbo shrimp coated in cream sauce. You'll be rushed out the door in under an hour, but you'll be happy and full.

Shh!

As expensive as San Francisco is, there are still off-the-radar joints that serve solid, affordable morsels — like Yamo *(3406 18th Street)*. This hole-in-the-wall, cash-only Burmese establishment is perfect for grabbing a quick, affordable, and satisfying meal before exploring the rest of the city. A word to the wise: don't leave without trying the house-made noodles and tasty tea-leaf salads. You won't regret it.

18TH STREET

GUERRERO STREET

VALENCIA STREET

SOUTH VAN NESS AVENUE

Mooch around
BI-RITE MARKET
Browse the aisles at this celebrated gourmet market for edible (and quaffable) souvenirs, all of which are produced in the Bay Area.

Swing by
CRAFTSMAN AND WOLVES
Arrive early at this popular pâtisserie, where pastries blur the lines between food and art. The Rebel Within muffin is a must-try.

20TH STREET

MISSION

*The Mission Burrito was created in **the Mission** in the 1960s. Now eaten across the US, it uses an extra-large tortilla and is jam-packed with rice.*

DOLORES STREET

Grab a coffee from
RITUAL COFFEE ROASTERS
Drop by this roastery for a seasonal espresso that lives up to improbable tasting notes like elderflower and persimmon.

VALENCIA STREET

MISSION STREET

*Immigrant families settled in the Mission from the 1940s through the 90s, and lots of their taquerias and cafés on **Valencia Street** still remain.*

24TH STREET

25TH STREET

Join a cooking class at
THE CIVIC KITCHEN
Home-cooking skills lacking? Fear not. Learn how to make savory soufflés or vegan meatballs at the Civic Kitchen.

0 meters 300
0 yards 300

**Rest up at
FLOUR + WATER**

Relax with a well-earned glass of wine and bowl of *raviolini* at this pantheon to little-known pastas.

A day sampling
food in the Mission

Neighborhoods don't get more dynamic than the Mission, where old-school taquerias stand side by side with neon-lit tattoo parlors and graffiti-sprayed cocktail bars. But talk to any resident and they'll tell you that it's the food scene that makes this 'hood so special. If you want to taste San Francisco in all its super-local and nerdy inventiveness (and you really should), the Mission can give you a taste of local flavors in a few blocks.

1. Bi-Rite Market
3639 18th Street;
The Mission;
www.biritemarket.com
///glow.stream.shell

2. Craftsman and Wolves
746 Valencia Street;
The Mission; www.
craftsman-wolves.com
///cheeks.wonderfully.flags

3. Ritual Coffee Roasters
1026 Valencia Street,
The Mission;
www.ritualroasters.com
///spit.spins.moving

4. The Civic Kitchen
2961 Mission Street,
The Mission; www.
civickitchensf.com
///pulse.comet.relate

5. Flour + Water
2401 Harrison Street,
The Mission; www.
flourandwater.com
///clap.toward.choice

DRINK

Cafés and bars are central to SF's social scene. Coffee is quaffed en route to work, wine is poured at after-work catch-ups, and elaborate cocktails toast the weekend.

Cocktail Joints

*The Bay Area invented the tiki bar in the 1930s, when
the US was in the clutches of the Depression and the
nearby South Pacific offered a sense of escape. Soak up
the chilled vibes at these classic cocktail joints.*

TRICK DOG

Map 4; 3010 20th Street, The Mission; ///when.snail.allow;
www.trickdogbar.com

There's nothing try-hard about Trick Dog. There's no table service
and the bartenders have that just-rolled-out-of-bed vibe. So it's not
what you'd expect from a "World's 50 Best Bars" mainstay – until you
start to sip, that is. The flavors are punchy and the concepts quirky,
with menus changing biannually (previous themes have included
Pantone shades and Dr Seuss). Cocktails don't get more tricksy.

PACIFIC COCKTAIL HAVEN

Map 1; 580 Sutter Street, Tendernob; ///editor.proof.books;
www.pacificcocktailsf.com

This low-key bar is a diamond in the rough amid the bus tours and
department stores of Union Square. The unmarked entrance is
subtle enough that it's missed by the hordes of nearby hotel guests,

leaving it to Downtown's after-work crowd and Tendernob locals (rents here attract a down-to-earth crowd, who lack a six-figure tech paycheck). Clever Pacific Island-tinged cocktails nod to SF's tiki heritage, and there are Japanese high-balls on tap.

» **Don't leave without** sipping the Leeward Negroni, a subtly tropical twist mixed with pandan cordial and coconut-washed Campari.

TRUE LAUREL

Map 4; 753 Alabama Street, The Mission; ///lasts.loyal.cult; www.truelaurelsf.com

It should come as no surprise that a bar from the drinks director of Lazy Bear *(p44)*, San Francisco's hyper-seasonal "dinner party" restaurant, is all about farm-to-glass sips. Visionary blends incorporate local flavors like laurel tincture and redwood tips, while zero percent options include non-alcoholic coffee liqueur with elderflower cordial. Cheers to that.

SMUGGLER'S COVE

Map 2; 650 Gough Street, Hayes Valley; ///lodge.trips.tilt; www.smugglerscovesf.com

Going behind Smuggler's nondescript door is like being teleported onto a *Pirates of the Caribbean* set. But this tiny tiki spot, anointed "best bar" by both the prestigious Spirited Awards and *SF Weekly* readers, is serious about tropical drinks. SF's craft cocktail geeks come for sips that stay true to the virtuoso recipes of the genre's 1950s heyday, when secretive bartenders wrote recipes in code.

Solo, Pair, Crowd

San Francisco is a "come-as-you-are" kind of city, making solo drinking unintimidating, date nights relaxing, and group hangs a blast.

FLYING SOLO

People-watch with a drink

Grab a tome from next door's iconic City Lights Bookstore, then head for the upstairs loft at North Beach saloon Vesuvio, which gives great views across busy Columbus Avenue below.

IN A PAIR

Canoodle over cocktails

Impress your other half with ABV, an award-winning bar in the Mission. Join locals at shared tables and choose from a list of 20+ original cocktails, including low ABV and non-alcoholic drinks.

FOR A CROWD

Raise a bowl to your pals

Hit up the outdoor terrace at tropical-themed Anina, where garrulous groups welcome the weekend with punch bowls.

WHITECHAPEL

Map 3; 600 Polk Street, Tenderloin; ///when.snail.allow; www.whitechapelsf.com

Few travelers venture into the Tenderloin, but SF's discerning night owls know that many of the city's most exciting bars are found here, including this gin-focused lounge. The green tiles and barrel-vaulted ceilings seem straight out of a London gin palace and the menu is just as gin-themed, with gin-flavored everything.

THE BEEHIVE

Map 4; 842 Valencia Street, The Mission; ///tower.slips.pump; www.thebeehivesf.com

It may seem like a quaint, unassuming watering hole, but this 1960s-inspired cocktail bar is anything but ordinary. Fun drinking game: take a slug each time you see a beehive-inspired piece of decor and drinkware. Going with a group? Get there before 11pm.

>> Don't leave without trying the Green Emanuelle – an amalgamation of Grey Goose, kiwi, soda, lime leaf, and elderflower liqueur.

LAST RITES

Map 2; 718 14th Street, Duboce Triangle; ///woods.horn.pilots; www.lastritesbar.com

Replacing grinning totems and pink umbrellas with vine-strangled skulls, Last Rites gives the tiki bar a darker spin. Even the drinks have more bite – tropical fruit flavors are blended with the likes of green chili liqueur. It's typically low-key: the regulars even bring their dogs.

Historic Boozers

*San Francisco's boozing and carousing reputation
dates back to the Gold Rush. Today, Wild West saloons
with swinging doors, Prohibition-era speakeasies, and
Beat bars make up the city's historic watering holes.*

LI PO COCKTAIL LOUNGE

**Map 1; 916 Grant Avenue, Chinatown; //first.mops.export;
www.lipolounge.com**

Join the end-of-the-night drinkers at this classic Chinatown dive bar.
A mainstay since 1937, it was beloved by Beat icons like Jack
Kerouac and Allen Ginsberg. Today, the cool crowds still head for
Li Po's neon Chinese lantern sign when they fancy an ultra-strength
"Chinese Mai Tai." An ode to the archetypal Bay Area cocktail, it's
spiked with a mysteriously vague "Chinese liqueur."

COMSTOCK SALOON

**Map 1; 155 Columbus Avenue, North Beach; ///closed.land.richer;
www.comstocksaloon.com**

Walking in here feels like traveling back in time to the days of the
Wild West. In fact, Comstock is the lone survivor of the Barbary
Coast, the notorious red light district that occupied this part of the city

during the Gold Rush. These days, it's less spit and sawdust than vintage wallpaper and fancy floor tiles, and gritty prospectors have been replaced by jazz fans, who come here for the free nightly sets.

» Don't leave without ordering from the food menu – the tater tot poutine is perfect for sobering up when you've had one too many.

BOURBON & BRANCH

Map 1; 501 Jones Street, Tenderloin; ///dreams.looked.trip;
www.bourbonandbranch.com

The Tenderloin's seedy rep harks back to the days of Prohibition, when it became SF's premier destination for speakeasies. Back then, 501 Jones Street was an illicit bar in a cigar shop basement. Nowadays, the unmarked door is still found beneath a subtle "Anti-Saloon League" sign, but the password is emailed to you with your reservation confirmation. Although snobbier San Franciscans give the Tenderloin (or TL) a wide berth, they make an exception for this secret slice of city history.

Can't get a rezzie at Bourbon & Branch? Head around the corner, where an unmarked door is not-so-subtly guarded by a bouncer. Inside, a small bar decked out like a library – no prizes for guessing the speakeasy's name – accepts walk-ins: unsurprisingly, the password is "books."

BUENA VISTA CAFE

Map 1; 2765 Hyde Street, Fisherman's Wharf; ///funds.vibe.person;
www.thebuenavista.com

It's a San Francisco rite of passage: an Irish coffee at the Buena Vista, where the boozy brew was first introduced to the United States in 1952. The cream-topped, whiskey-spiked coffees soon became as much of a city staple as sourdough bread and Dungeness crab. Locals still love a steaming goblet of the good stuff, and when the Super Bowl's on, the bar can sell 6,000 in a day. The place is pure nostalgia, from bartenders in white jackets, to cable cars running outside. Good for when parents are visiting.

TWIN PEAKS TAVERN

Map 2; 401 Castro Street, The Castro; ///items.kind.parade;
www.twinpeakstavern.com

You can't miss always-buzzing Twin Peaks, right on the corner of major thoroughfares Castro and Market. A rainbow flag by the entrance welcomes patrons, who sit at the full-length glass windows of this,

Try it!
MONDAY NIGHT MIXOLOGY

Want to wow your friends with your liquor knowledge and skills? The Alembic *(www. alembicsf.com)* runs great classes on the history and process of whiskey. Better yet, you'll make four whiskey-based cocktails.

the country's first out-and-proud LGBTQ+ bar (having first thrown open its doors with gay abandon in 1972). Some call it the "Gay Cheers": the sort of place you settle in for long chats and cheap drinks.

TONGA ROOM & HURRICANE BAR

Map 1; 950 Mason Street, Nob Hill; ///asserts.vines.chained;
www.tongaroom.com

Yes, it's bizarre that an otherwise refined grande dame hotel has an utterly berserk tiki lounge in the basement. But remember: the Bay Area is very proud of its artisan tiki cocktail-making, which harks back to the 1930s. Drawing mates, dates, and befuddled hotel guests since 1945, the Fairmont's over-the-top tropical bar includes a twice-hourly "thunderstorm," and a band playing from a barge floating in the pool.

» Don't leave without sharing a classic Zombie cocktail, made to the original, ultra-strong recipe, dating from 1934.

WILD SIDE WEST

Map 4; 424 Cortland Avenue, Bernal Heights; ///hints.belts.left;
www.wildsidewest.com

The Bay Area's longest-surviving lesbian bar was an illicit revolutionary in its time, and the likes of Janis Joplin played pool behind its protective leather curtain in the 1960s. Ten years later, it moved to its current home in Bernal Heights, and was welcomed by protestors throwing broken toilets through the window. Today, those toilets double as flower pots in the backyard "magic garden", where guys and girls of all orientations spend long afternoons sipping pints.

Wine Bars

*With the Napa and Sonoma winelands almost in sight
of the Golden Gate Bridge, it should come as no
surprise that San Franciscans like to drink local,
organic, and biodynamic at any given opportunity.*

UNION LARDER

Map 1; 1945 Hyde Street, Russian Hill; ///sound.lucky.forget;
www.unionlarder.com

Ultra-chilled Union Larder is whatever you need it to be, but if you're
in the mood for a well-informed wine bar that serves 40 varieties of
wine by the glass you've hit the jackpot. Chummy servers are on
hand to guide you through the Bay Area's best wine as old friends
catch up over a glass of Chardonnay (or two).

PRESS CLUB

Map 3; 20 Yerba Buena Lane, SoMa; ///round.fake.bumpy;
www.pressclubsf.com

San Francisco doesn't really do dressing up, but if you want to throw
on your finest, come to this clubby wine bar. The sleek, subterranean
space – all concrete and walnut wood – is where a mixed bag of
older suits, fleece-clad start-up CEOs, and female friends gather for

If you're really looking to party, things hot up here on the weekend, with live DJs and dancing into the wee early hours.

on-tap wines and seasonal small bites. Whites and reds lean heavily on California and West Coast vintages. They also organize top-notch events with artisan vintners.

RESOLUTE

Map 1; 678 Geary Street, Tenderloin; ///slides.rungs.rear; www.resolutesf.com

It's testament to how far the Tenderloin has come that there's a wine bar of this calibre on Geary. Residents can't quite believe their luck in having Resolute as their local, as they recline on wraparound white-and-blue banquettes, sup on boutique, small-batch vinos, and savor the kitchen's crispy *pissaladières* (French-style, thin-crust pizza). It's the kind of place to bring a good friend or impress a date.

AMELIE

Map 1; 1754 Polk Street, Nob Hill; ///rots.cape.leaned; www.ameliewinebar.com

Cute and cosy Amelie's decor may seem straight out of Paris, but the crowd is oh-so-San-Francisco – a lively cohort of folk psyched by the $10 happy-hour wine flights (until 7pm). The wine list is split into old world and new world, repping Napa and Sonoma along-side OGs like Bordeaux and the Loire Valley.

>> **Don't leave without** wandering down the hill for a post-vino pick-me-up at Bob's Donuts – the frosted apple fritters are incredible.

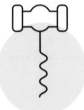

Liked by the locals

"High Treason is a very San Francisco wine bar because anyone can come in and be comfortable. There are 20 different glasses that cost under $10: we know wine doesn't have to be expensive to be good."

JOHN VUONG, CO-OWNER OF HIGH TREASON

HIGH TREASON

Map 5; 443 Clement Street, Inner Richmond; ///career.foam.supply;
www.hightreasonsf.com

This narrow neighborhood joint has fast become an "it" destination for everyone from restaurant insiders to young families. The appeal is that it's so accessible: there's no judgment, whether your glass costs $9 or $19. It's for those who like their wine down-to-earth.

CALIFORNIA WINE MERCHANT

Map 5; 2113 Chestnut Street, Marina District; ///salon.drop.fumes;
www.californiawinemerchant.com

Stocking everything from rare passito wines (made from dried grapes) to more standard reds, California Wine Merchant really is a one-stop-shop for all your wine wants and wishes. Overwhelmed? Owner Greg O'Flynn and his staff are impressively knowledgeable.

» Don't leave without sampling a glass of the Lost Angel 2017 Pinot Noir, which is a crowd-favorite for its cherry notes and hints of vanilla.

TERROIR

Map 3; 1116 Folsom Street, SoMa; ///candy.chops.slide;
www.terroirsf.com

It looks more like a hipster coffee shop than one of the most influential wine bars in the country, with its reclaimed wood communal counters and plastic stools. But make no mistake: Terroir became an American wine world hero by championing natural and organic wines well before they were on trend.

Breweries and Beer Bars

Keeping up with Northern California's 800 vineyards are more than 300 craft breweries. Sample homegrown brews in SF's new-school cool taprooms and good old-fashioned pubs.

BAREBOTTLE BREWING

Map 4; 1525 Cortland Avenue, Bernal Heights; ///door.spice.bliss; www.barebottle.com

Friends line communal benches and toast to the weekend, parents jiggle pushchairs and sink frothy pints, and couples compete at games of corn hole. This is Barebottle Brewing, a social hub where beer lovers meet to sip creative brews, named things like Honey Boo Boo.

MAGNOLIA BREWING

Map 2; 1398 Haight Street, Haight-Ashbury; ///sample.lobby.ruled; www.magnoliabrewing.com

Magnolia Brewing has been making craft beer since the 1990s, when stout was still something your dad drank and no one had even heard of IPA. Forgo today's tropes of drinking from designer cans in industrial warehouses and take your friends to this quintessential San Franciscan Victorian, in the heart of hippie Haight-Ashbury, for traditional English-style beers brewed using California-farmed hops.

21ST AMENDMENT BREWERY & RESTAURANT

Map 3; 563 2nd Street, South Beach; ///really.bottle.agents; www.21st-amendment.com

Both floors at this warehouse-style brewery are pretty consistently packed. During the week, it's where the SOMA after-work crowd comes to let loose; on the weekend, it's baseball-mad families and sports fans – the pub is right next to Oracle Park, the home stadium of the San Francisco Giants, after all. Intimate it's not, but when it comes to the beer, these guys are among the city's finest indie brewers.

>> Don't leave without trying the "Hell or High Watermelon" wheat beer, brewed with real watermelons – it's summer in a sip.

FORT POINT VALENCIA

Map 4; 742 Valencia Street, The Mission; ///deflection.detail.oath; www.fortpointbeer.com

Named for the fort under the Golden Gate Bridge, Fort Point Valencia has brought the traditional beer hall into the 21st century. The brightly painted walls, neon signs, and preponderance of plants all yell "hipster," and the clientele has an above-average count of sleeve tattoos and fancy backpacks. By day, it's mellow enough for the odd MacBook-tapping freelancer. By night, it's a whole other ball game.

ANCHOR PUBLIC TAPS

Map 3; 495 De Haro Street, Potrero Hill; ///jumpy.exact dining;
www.anchorbrewing.com

Young coders love this place for (a) creating something to do in Potrero Hill, (b) hosting random events like movie nights and booksales, and (c) having bocce courts in the parking lot. Beer aficionados put up with this Silicon Valley crowd because this bar is the home of Anchor, the original San Francisco craft beer that was founded in 1896. Okay, it's now owned by the Japanese giant Sapporo, but this spot keeps the spirit of independence, brewing an exclusive collection of beers solely for Public Taps' patrons.

» Don't leave without sampling street bites from the on-site food trucks, which serve anything from seafood salads to Cali-Mexican tacos.

BLACK HAMMER BREWING

Map 3; 544 Bryant Street, SoMa; ///privately.handed.barn;
www.blackhammerbrewing.com

Building community in a district that resembles a building site more than a neighborhood is no easy task, yet BHB pulls it off. This ultramodern taproom has become the ultimate gathering place for SoMa's workers, families, and dog-owners due to its funky yet friendly aesthetic – think retractable factory windows, rotating art exhibits, and ironic disco balls. But it's not just BHB's decor that has won so many fans; it's the daily changing, small-batch beers that have people coming back again and again. Styles range from Norwegian ales to gluten-reduced stouts, and there are non-alcoholic options for teetotalers and jars of dog treats for little

Order in a sourdough pizza or open-faced sandwich from Goat Hill Pizza, just over the road from BHB. four-legged patrons. Getting peckish but don't want to leave? The taproom is cool with you ordering in food from local restaurants – in fact, it's encouraged.

THE SYCAMORE

Map 4; 2140 Mission Street, Mission Dolores;
///under.oven.mouse; www.thesycamoresf.com

After an afternoon spent sunbathing and picnicking atop the green grass at Dolores Park, 20- and 30-somethings in-the-know head to this gastropub. Here, strangers-turned-newfound-friends sup on beers and strike up impromptu games of Twister and dominoes on the huge sun-soaked patio. With such an inclusive atmosphere, it's the perfect choice for solo travelers. Be warned: the drinks are as stiff as Karl (the nickname for the Bay Area's perennial fog) is thick, so soak up the alcohol with the Sycamore's famous fried cheese curds.

THE MONK'S KETTLE

Map 4; 3141 16th Street, Mission Dolores; ///manker.bind.pans;
www.monkskettle.com

Saddled between the Castro and Mission Dolores, this cosy gastropub specializes in local and Belgian brews. The bartenders and servers are happy to advise on which beer goes with which dish – or which one you'd enjoy on its own – but there's not one bad brew on the menu. Keep abreast of the live music program on social media and bring a group of friends for beats and beers.

Rooftop Bars

There's a bizarre dearth of rooftop bars in San Francisco, and those that do exist are mostly Downtown, shunning Bay views for skyscrapers. Nevertheless, there are a few hidden gems.

CHARMAINE'S ROOFTOP BAR & LOUNGE

Map 3; 1100 Market Street, Mid-Market; ///shares.entry.square; www.properhotel.com

The closest thing in San Francisco to a "see and be seen" spot, Charmaine's is such a rarity that the line often stretches down the block. No small achievement in scrappy Mid-Market, which, despite being home to the Twitter and Uber HQs, is more than a little rough around the edges. Not that you'll notice once you're up here, lounging on a black-and-white couch by a crackling fire pit.

DIRTY HABIT

Map 3; 12 4th Street, SoMa; ///plays.help.dads; www.dirtyhabitsf.com

After-work groups head straight for the roof deck at the back of this fifth-floor bar, found inside Hotel Zelos. But make no mistake – it's not the views that draw people to Dirty Habit (unless they really dig the sides of buildings) but the vibe. Here, friends and co-workers loosen their collars and kick back with punch bowls. And about those punch bowls: less Kool Aid and vodka, more tarragon and Lillet Rose. Think slick without being chichi.

EL TECHO DE LOLINDA

Map 4; 2516 Mission Street, The Mission; ///silk.richer.serve;
www.eltechosf.com

If the sun is shining, you'd better get here early, because every Mission hipster will be headed this way. Located on top of Argentine steakhouse Lolinda, El Techo is the perfect place to indulge in some day-drinking, with its easy-breezy vibe and Latin American street snacks. Take a date, order margaritas, and soak up the quintessential San Franciscan view of boxy houses spilling down green hills.

620 JONES

Map 1; 620 Jones Street, Tenderloin; ///leans.sleeps.person;
www.620-jones.com

Friends tell friends, who tell yet more friends, about this outdoor patio, which is so well-hidden down an alley that you could live next to it and not notice it until the day that someone whispers the words "620 Jones." With views of ornate apartment buildings, the regular crowd of young professionals, students, and the occasional drag queen always makes for a party.

>> Don't leave without taking in the view of the 70-ft (20-m) golden brain mural, a tribute to the Tenderloin by street artist Believe in People.

TOP OF THE MARK

Map 1; 999 California Street, Nob Hill; ///boot.bells.shield;
www.intercontinentalmarkhopkins.com

All right, it's not alfresco, but this 19th-floor, self-professed "sky lounge" does have floor-to-ceiling, 360-degree views. It's one of those "go there at least once" destinations, a retro-cool kind of place to sip martinis (or a 0 percent cocktail) and gawp at views across the neighborhood's wedding-cake mansions to Alcatraz Island and the Golden Gate Bridge. Sure, you'll see tourists, but locals also love it for special occasions, even ditching their hoodies and sneakers for proper attire.

ROOFTOP 25

Map 3; 25 Lusk Street, China Basin; ///focal.slave.vanish; www.25lusk.com

Without the airs and graces of its counterparts, Rooftop 25 is the place to bring friends when you actually want to be able to have a conversation. Row upon row of tables sit underneath twinkling

You don't have to be a guest at the Marriott to access the hotel bar, The View Lounge *(www. marriott.co.uk)*. And yeah, okay, it's under cover, but we swear the views from this Art Deco-inspired bar are gorgeous. Don your glad rags and nab a seat by the enormous arched window, the bar's focal point, which looks out onto Downtown. The views are especially lovely at dusk, and best enjoyed with a glass of California Zinfadel.

lights. There's food, too: great pizzas are churned out by an oakwood-fired oven and hot dogs are served in a pretzel bun. The perfect sustenance to refuel during a proper catchup.

MAD OAK

Map 6; 135 12th Street, Oakland; ///radar.itself.owls; www.madoakbar.com

This laid-back outdoor beer garden and rooftop bar is a hot spot for young San Franciscans and office workers hunting for happy hour. Join them for beers and an evening of cheering at the game on the outdoor TVs, or gather the gang for a game of cornhole (Mad Oak's favorite garden game). With outdoor heaters and a kitchen serving restaurant-worthy grub, it's the ideal spot for a long summer night, or a date if you don't mind the lively atmosphere.

B RESTAURANT & BAR

Map 3; 720 Howard Street, Yerba Buena;
///accent.coherent.tennis; www.bsanfrancisco.com

Nestled atop the Moscone Convention Center, B is a wonderland of views, dollar oysters, and seasonal cocktails. Patrons – a melting pot of tech workers, groups of animated girlfriends, and suited-up businessmen – sit out on the modern terrazzo after a hard day's work and watch the sun set over Yerba Buena Gardens, drinks in hand. Suffice to say that B makes for a perfect upscale, yet casual backdrop for a date night.

» Don't leave without trying the Paloma – a citrus-heavy drink with a hint of elderflower. The perfect summer's drink.

Coffee Shops

*Every San Franciscan has a favorite local roaster.
These indie enterprises tend to work closely with
fair-trade farms, and compete for creativity when
it comes to amping up a latte.*

TROUBLE COFFEE COMPANY

**Map 6; 4033 Judah Street, Outer Sunset; ///factor.cups.marble;
www.trouble.coffee**

Sunset folks won't consider anywhere else for a latte, even if it
means waiting on the driftwood bench outside for 20 minutes, while
being buffeted by glacial gales blowing over from Ocean Beach.
Why all the fuss? Besides the good java, the cinnamon sugar toast
plated up here is the stuff of legend (there's even an episode of *This
American Life* dedicated to it).

PHILZ COFFEE

**Map 4; 3101 24th Street, The Mission; ///sketch.rats.good;
www.philzcoffee.com**

It's a regional chain now, but the original Philz, on 24th Street, remains
a Mission favorite. Old dudes and young techies bring their laptops,
settling into beaten-up couches under a sky-painted ceiling; folks in

tie-dye and grey pigtails idly chat with whoever else is waiting in line. Be warned that only a local can look at the coffee menu without breaking into an intimidated sweat. Swallow your pride and ask the baristas for guidance: they'll make the best damn cup you've ever had.

» **Don't leave without** ordering the signature mint mojito (creamy iced coffee with fresh mint) – unbelievably refreshing.

CONTRABAND COFFEE BAR

Map 1; 1415 Larkin Street, Nob Hill; ///nerve.dots.violin; www.contrabandcoffeebar.com

Not even the obnoxiously loud punk tunes blasted through Contraband's speakers can keep Mac-toting freelancers from staying here until closing time. Maybe it's the signature sage and rosemary cappuccinos, or perhaps it's that this is the hippest place in the old-money Nob Hill neighborhood. Need a break from the noise? There's always the sidewalk tables outside.

ANDYTOWN COFFEE ROASTERS

Map 6; 3629 Taraval, Outer Sunset; ///sailor.create.also; www.andytownsf.com

Just two words can send SF's coffee set into the throes of ecstasy: "Snowy Plover." This is Andytown's trademark – a shot of house-roasted espresso, mixed with brown sugar, then poured into a glass of San Pellegrino water, and finished with homemade whipped cream. The café is only a block from Ocean Beach, so if it's too cold to sit still on the patio, take your cup to go and stroll the sand instead.

SIGHTGLASS COFFEE

Map 3; 270 7th Street, SoMa; ///panel.cool.local;
www.sightglasscoffee.com

If the hipster coffee movement had a HQ, it would be Sightglass. Inside the massive, light-filled factory space, beanie-wearing freelancers drink single-origin espressos at the slim bar, furiously tapping away at their laptops. Moving up a floor to the mezzanine, start-ups hold team meetings under the lofty, wood-beamed ceilings, breaking to help themselves to the build-your-own affogato bar (where flash-chilled coffees on tap are also served). It's just too easy to while away an afternoon here, getting jazzed on the finest produce of indie fincas, and feeling pretty cool at the same time.

» Don't leave without sipping a sparkling cascara shrub, Sightglass's own health drink, flavored with the dried skins of coffee cherries.

BLUE BOTTLE COFFEE

Map 1; Ferry Building, Embarcadero; ///gender.last.bumpy;
www.bluebottlecoffee.com

It's a fairly typical story around these parts: Oakland-based freelance musician who's super-nerdy about coffee starts selling his own meticulously roasted brews. Twenty years later, he's built a sustainably sourced, third-wave coffee empire with outposts in Tokyo and Seoul, and has a cult following of caffeine-addicted fans. And that's Blue Bottle Coffee. Whatever you order here, be it an outrageously silky cappuccino or a chicory-spiked, New Orleans-style iced coffee, take it outside and sip with a view of the Bay Bridge. Coffee and scenery – what more could you want?

Liked by the locals

"San Francisco's coffee scene is diverse and robust, but most importantly, it's sustainable, too. Blue Bottle is most proud to call this community home because of how we all stand up for what we know to be just."

JASON MILLER, BARISTA AT BLUE BOTTLE COFFEE

An evening of cocktails in
the Tenderloin

It's scrappy, it's ragged around the edges, but the Tenderloin is home to the most exciting 'Frisco bars. This isn't new; the area was notorious for its speakeasies in the 1920s, not to mention burlesque houses and gambling dens. The 'hood maintains a reputation for crime and general squalor, but cheaper rents make it possible for young, creative bartenders to set up shop here. Whether you like beautifully crafted cocktails, or prefer your liquor neat, the bars of the Tenderloin have something to sip and savor.

TENDERNOB

**Have a nightcap at
THE SARATOGA**
End at this glamorous bi-level cocktail lounge to sip a Chartreuse: there's an incredible collection of dusty vintage bottles.

1. Benjamin Cooper
398 Geary Street,
Tenderloin; www.
benjamincooper.com
///state.turns.views

3. The Saratoga
1000 Larkin Street,
Tendernob; www.
thesaratogasf.com
///corner.actors.wide

2. Rye
688 Geary Street,
Tenderloin; www.ryesf.com
///noting.quiet.privately

POLK

STREET

LARKIN

Bourbon and Branch ///tapes.keeps.album

Black Hawk ///rises.diner.pound

TURK   STREET

JONES STREET

TAYLOR STREET

MASON STREET

Relish a drink in RYE

The clue's in the name:
it's all about whiskey at Rye.
Study the extensive menu
and enjoy a dram or a
whiskey-based cocktail.

POST STREET

Union Square

TENDERLOIN

GEARY STREET

Feel sophisticated at BENJAMIN COOPER

Find the unmarked entrance on
Mason Street, where dimly lit stairs
lead down to this sexy bar. Slurp
oysters and sip an original cocktail.

O'FARRELL STREET

LEAVENWORTH STREET

HYDE STREET

ELLIS STREET

EDDY STREET

*Speakeasies often asked
for a password in the
20s, and some bars still
uphold this tradition; for*
Bourbon & Branch *it's
"books."*

MASON STREET

MARKET STREET

5TH STREET

TURK STREET

The **Black Hawk**
*jazz bar opened in 1949
and, for 14 years, let kids
in provided they didn't
drink booze (and sat
behind chicken wire).*

6TH STREET

SOMA

MARKET STREET

CIVIC CENTER

| 0 meters | 200 |
| 0 yards | 200 |

SHOP

Come the weekend and San Franciscans have one thing in mind: shopping. Nothing beats perusing a local store, chatting to the owner, and leaving with a new treasure.

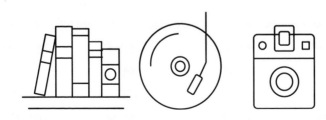

US Design

San Francisco's sustainably minded shoppers browse upstart fashion labels and small independent stores for unique, locally designed and Bay-Area-made clothes and accessories.

BETABRAND

Map 4; 780 Valencia Street, The Mission;
///vision.estate.rescue; www.betabrand.com

Where do San Franciscans go for unique threads? Betabrand, a self-professed fashion industry disruptor, where all the designs are crowdsourced, put to a public vote, and produced if enough are pre-ordered. The sell-out pieces are the "dress pant yoga pants" – work-appropriate trousers manufactured to feel as comfy as your favorite loungewear. How very San Franciscan.

LOCAL TAKE

Map 2; 3979B 17th Street, The Castro;
///layers.poet.atomic; www.localtakesf.com

Surprisingly, there are always more locals than tourists browsing in this great gift shop, which only sells products made by Bay Area artists and designers. We're partial to the graphic tees that depict

San Franciscan neighborhoods as different types of bicycle. They also do incredibly cute babywear plus a great range of equal rights accessories. We'll take the Ruth Bader Ginsburg pin.

MARINE LAYER

Map 2; 498 Hayes Street, Hayes Valley;
///pasta.mixed.hike; www.marinelayer.com

San Francisco's dressed-down residents perfect their Cali-casual look at Marine Layer. Everything from the cosy hoodies to the stylish dresses are made with custom fabrics and manufactured here or in LA. The signature soft T-shirt, which is woven from recycled beechwood, needs to be felt to be believed. Though at $100 for three they need to be comfortable.

» **Don't leave without** trying the "Mystery Tee" vending machine at the back of the store, which dispenses half-priced tops at random.

GRAVEL & GOLD

Map 4; 3266 21st Street, The Mission;
///junior.search.weeks; www.gravelandgold.com

Where does a Cali girl outfit her wardrobe? This women-owned collective sells a cornucopia of locally designed and made goodies: original womenswear, funky socks, jewelry, plus art, greeting cards, homeware, and some extremely adult coloring books. The shop hosts an interesting schedule of events, too. Think non-toxic beauty workshops, magical dreaming seminars, and the occasional transformational healing sound bath. Move over, Goop.

TIGERLILY PERFUMERY

Map 4; 973 Valencia Street, The Mission;
///sits.noises.afford; www.tigerlilyperfumery.com

Idiosyncratic San Franciscans don't want to smell like everyone else.
Hence this small-batch perfume boutique, where vintage bureaus
are topped with bottles of all-natural, locally made fragrances. Spritz
yourself in Mission-based Bruno Fazzolari's color-inspired perfumes
or Latin American-owned Laromatica's bourbon-influenced scent.

NOOWORKS

Map 4; 395 Valencia Street, The Mission;
///ends.groups.juices; www.nooworks.com

Love a bold print? Then you'll love Nooworks. Expect jumpsuits galore:
possibly bright-pink and covered in bananas, or purple and dotted
with dalmatian-like snakes The store partners with a rotating cast
of female artists, so you'll need to go back to see the latest stock.
» Don't leave without pondering a potential buy while sipping an
artisanal tea at the excellent Samovar Tea Bar, located just next door.

TIMBUK2 FACTORY STORE

Map 4; 587 Shotwell Street, The Mission;
///mirror.vets.beams; www.timbuk2.com

Techies and utilitarians looking for durable accessories love Timbuk2
for its fashionable, long-lasting backpacks and messenger bags in
various muted shades. They also carry a pretty good range of
beanies and panel caps, if you're after some new headgear.

Liked by the locals

"It's always a joy to see the look on a customer's face when they realize they've not only found a perfume that smells amazing on their skin, but one that no one else knows about yet."

ANTONIA KOHL, OWNER OF TIGERLILY PERFUMERY

Record Stores

Put Spotify and iTunes aside for a minute. To keep it real, join San Francisco's punks and mods, jazzheads and club kids between aisles of vinyl, swapping stories as you leaf through records.

ROOKY RICARDO'S RECORDS

Map 2; 419 Haight Street, Lower Haight;
///vital.unable.bids; www.rookyricardos.com

Soul and funk fans could – and do – spend all day at Rooky Ricardo's, a throwback store decked out in vintage signs and lights. They thumb through the sounds of the 1950s, 60s and 70s, gabbing about the unheard gems of British mod and American soul. Pull up a stool at the listening station to hear owner Dick's picks before you commit.

NOISE

Map 6; 3427 Balboa Street, Outer Richmond;
///lower.vibes.estate; www.sanfrancisconoise.com

The family that owns this record-store-meets-art-gallery have been residents of Outer Richmond for more than 30 years. That makes the store a real neighborhood spot, where people pop in for a gossip as much as for the chance of unearthing an unsung

Jazz bands play at Noise every Sunday, from 2pm. Roll up to join a mix of Outer Richmond old-timers and jazz heads.

gem. The works on the walls, all by local artists, are also for sale. Be sure to tap whoever's working for some stories about old-school San Francisco: that's what this place is all about.

AMOEBA MUSIC
Map 2; 1855 Haight Street, Haight-Ashbury;
///loving.shares.test; www.amoeba.com

This huge store in the heart of Haight-Ashbury was a bowling alley in a previous life. Those born in the naughties might consider it a veritable antique shop, with aisle upon aisle of vinyl, CDs, DVDs and Blu-Rays, turntables, and posters. It's a stubbornly analog rebuff to digitized San Francisco, and we're big fans.

>> Don't leave without catching one of the store's many free live shows, featuring up-and-coming bands and legends alike.

GROOVES INSPIRALLED VINYL
Map 2; 1797 Market Street, Hayes Valley;
///fled.such.mercy; www.groovesrecords.com

In the 1960s, Ray Andersen designed light shows for bands playing at The Fillmore, including Jimi Hendrix, Pink Floyd, and The Grateful Dead. But his real passion was this record shop, the upshot of his own enormous, genre-spanning vinyl collection. Today, music lovers from far and wide make for the distinctive spiral sign to flip through the famously cluttered trays, now overseen by Andersen's daughter, Sunny.

ORIGINALS VINYL

Map 2; 701 Fillmore Street, Alamo Square;
///filled.open.smooth; www.originalsvinyl.com

This independent spot casts off the whole vintage, dusty record shop feel in favor of modern minimalism: all light wood, potted plants, and clean lines. The small inventory is meticulously organized, and, alongside used funk, reggae, and blues LPs, favors fresh hip-hop pressings and soul and jazz reissues. The owners, brothers Dominic and Matt, started collecting in their DJ days in the mid-1990s, and are often around to share nerdy rare record chat.

STRANDED

Map 4; 1055 Valencia Street, The Mission;
///soap.cakes.slowly; www.strandedrecords.com

The reincarnation of Mission district darling Aquarius Records, Stranded carries a well-curated selection of records that you generally wouldn't find in a regular record store (we're talking post-punk, avant-garde, and experimental). And we can't forget the relentlessly

Try it!
SPIN DECKS

Always wanted to DJ? Book classes with DJ Lamont *(www.fingersnaps.net)*, who has been playing records for almost 50 years. Pick from a 1-hour Mission Spin masterclass or 2-hour One Hit Wonder.

smiley staff, who are only too happy to point you in the direction of a stellar record. Visiting Oakland? Swing by the East Bay outpost to check out the selection there.

THRILLHOUSE RECORDS

Map 4; 3422 Mission Street, Bernal Heights;
///target.bucket.composers; www.thrillhouserecords.com

Some think Bay Area punk begins and ends with Green Day, but this graffiti- and sticker-strewn, volunteer-run record store would beg to differ. The nonprofit is all about punk on vinyl, has a dedicated "Bay Area bands" section, and even hosts a Cyberpunk Cinema series at nearby pub The Knockout, with drink specials and free popcorn. Check its Facebook page for updates on all the latest events.

» **Don't leave without** playing 1980s arcade games on Thrillhouse's free-to-play machine, while sharing a beer with whoever's working.

VINYL DREAMS

Map 2; 593 Haight Street, Lower-Haight; ///dull.gather.free;
www.vinyldreamssf.com

Vinyl Dreams is beloved for many things: its charming signage, well-versed staff, and dedication to supporting local artists. The snug, indie record store specializes in house, techno, disco, and electronica, but the catalog of media – which also includes a small list of CDs and cassettes – spans the gamut. Don't forget to check out the "secondhand jams" for some pre-owned records; you might just find the tune that you've been looking for at a bottom-dollar price.

Home Touches

Local makers, small-scale production, and hand-crafted pieces define SF design. The aesthetic is shorthand for the Bay Area way: fun and relaxed, beautiful in its simplicity, but finely made.

GENERAL STORE

Map 6; 4035 Judah Street, Outer Sunset; ///tools.exist.fats;
www.shop-generalstore.com

It doesn't get more Californian than Outer Sunset's General Store, where everything has that wonderful rustic and organic feel that the Bay Area is known for. Artisanal pieces include everything from woven baskets and cotton blankets to bamboo utensils and beeswax candles – all the kind of stuff that's easy to pack. And it's beautifully laid out too, like a chocolate box of treasures for the home.

HEATH CERAMICS

Map 4; 2900 18th Street, The Mission; ///hiding.port.tigers;
www.heathceramics.com

While tourists wedge themselves into Heath Ceramics' tiny Ferry Building location, locals stride around this massive Mission showroom. Best known for minimal dinnerware in distinctive glazes, these Bay

Area potters are considered one of America's last great design-led manufacturers. You can even spot their stuff at New York's MoMA. Doubling as a working tile factory and sewing studio, this space also sells home decor, kitchen and tabletop pieces, and leather totes.

» Don't leave without browsing the adjoining Heath newsstand and coffee shop, which stocks an interesting mix of independent magazines.

KENNETH WINGARD

Map 2; 2319 Market Street, The Castro; ///leave.organ.cubes; www.kennethwingard.com

When not appearing as the home decor expert on the Hallmark channel's *Home & Family*, Kenneth Wingard is at home in San Francisco, with his husband and three kids, running this Castro store. One of the area's too-few Black-owned businesses, it's filled with Wingard's fun and colorful, mid-century-inspired designs, with everything from lamps and vases to cushions and table linens.

Only open on Fridays and Saturdays (and by appointment), Leah Harmatz's Field Theory (*www.fieldtheorydesign.com*) shop and studio is an SF design dream. It's a peaceful haven, hidden away in a residential area where locals take time to browse the minimalist designs, and chat to Harmatz. Keep an eye out on Instagram for irregular pop-up events such as tarot workshops, floral design classes, and dining experiences.

MARCH

Map 5; 3075 Sacramento Street, Pacific Heights;
///drain.precautions.tags; www.marchsf.com

If you want to at least give off the impression that you're a proficient chef, then cookware shop March is the store for you. Here you can splash out on gorgeous crockery, canisters, and glassware, plus various cookbooks – perfect coffee table fodder if nothing else. In-store food events offer tips for home cooking and, more importantly, tastings.

» Don't leave without ducking into Rickshaw Bagworks, a block away, to check out its super-colorful, handmade messenger and duffle bags.

JAY JEFFERS — THE STUDIO

Map 1; 1035 Post Street, Tendernob; ///skin.throw.patio; www.jayjeffers.com

Jay Jeffers is a local interiors maven known for outfitting luxury pads, from Lake Tahoe to Napa. You wouldn't expect to find his glamour collection of California-made furniture here, in the gritty Tendernob, but Jeffers has been a big believer in the area for years and his Post Street studio is a cool setting for his scene-stealing home goods. Note opening hours are erratic, but you can make an appointment.

BABOO

Map 3; 101 Henry Adams Street # 335 SFDC, Design District;
///piper.spoke.secret; www.baboosf.com

Marketed as a place to find "off the beaten path" pieces of decor, BaBoo's commitment to both craftsmanship and community is treasured by locals looking to put a unique stamp on their space.

While BaBoo supports SF creatives, it also stocks goods from relatively unknown international brands, so you're bound to find something that matches your style. The geometric furnishings, chair swings, and modern pop-art pieces are popular purchases.

MCGUIRE FURNITURE

Map 3; 2 Henry Adams Street #333, Design District;
///deals.bowls.aware; www.mcguirefurniture.com

This self-styled "California-casual" design showroom is all about handcrafted furniture that'll last for a lifetime. If you're not quite ready to commit to a big buy, and don't have green to spare, there are tempting mirrors, floor lamps, and cocktail tables. But, beware, this is the sort of place that gives out prices on request. Ikea, it ain't.

ZOZI'S LOFT

Map 3; 249 9th Street, SoMa; ///shine.income.client; www.zozisloft.com

This local store is one of the rare mercantile establishments that's grown into a community place. SoMa's residents gather for a myriad of events in the loft, including – of all things – an annual Christmas party. Featuring over 100 furniture manufacturers, Zozi's Loft carries a huge array of living, dining, and bedroom pieces, as well as lighting accessories. Worried about transporting your new favorite chair home? Zozi's offers in-store shipping for those items too big to put in a carry-on. We love it for the fact that it exhibits and sells artworks by independent San Franciscan artists, with much of the profit going straight back into the artists' hands.

Book Nooks

San Franciscans are better known for writing code than poems nowadays, but once upon a time the city was a hotbed of anti-establishment creatives. Find traces of that literary legacy in the city's bookstores.

GREEN APPLE BOOKS

Map 5; 506 Clement Street, Inner Richmond; ///humble.hello.steep; www.greenapplebooks.com

You'll first spot this community cornerstone by the folks rifling through the sidewalk stacks. Inside, the place is a creaky-staired pleasure dome, piled high with new and used tomes. Keep an eye out for the store's many regulars, as well as events with literary heavyweights, like Lisa Taddeo.

CITY LIGHTS BOOKSELLERS & PUBLISHERS

Map 1; 261 Columbus Avenue, North Beach; ///drill.emerge.rust; www.citylights.com

City Lights has been ground zero for SF's iconoclasts ever since it got landed with an obscenity trial for publishing Allen Ginsberg's *Howl* back in 1952. The poem defined the Beat generation and forever linked City Lights with San Francisco counterculture. Books are filed under topics like "Anarchism and Class War," and weekly events discuss the likes of a nuclear-free future.

» Don't leave without giving a donation – small or large – to help this Bay Area landmark to keep selling literature to the masses.

DOG EARED BOOKS

Map 4; 900 Valencia Street, The Mission; ///smug.casual.whips; www.dogearedbooks.com

This bookstore survived Valencia Street's gentrification thanks to its dedicated regulars, who consider this satisfyingly stuffed store a comforting glimmer of the literary San Francisco that once was. There's a bit of everything among the new and used, but expect special attention to the obscure. Handwritten signs split shelves into offbeat interests, such as "Druids, Drugs, and Secret Societies."

BOUND TOGETHER ANARCHIST COLLECTIVE BOOKSTORE

Map 2; 1369 Haight Street, Haight-Ashbury; ///stud.skirt.divisions; www.boundtogetherbooks.wordpress.com

The spirit of counterculture lives on at this volunteer-run, "radical literature" bookstore, in the heart of the hippie Haight district. A small, poster-plastered space, it's crammed with books on underground and anarchist thought, and hosts speaker events, panels, and discussion groups. Best of all, some of its proceeds go to the Prisoners Literature Project, which provides prisoners with books.

Liked by the locals

"Black Bird looks different to other bookstores so that you can find what you didn't know you were looking for. It's a place to open up a new idea or thought."

KATHRYN GRANTHAM,
OWNER OF BLACK BIRD BOOKSTORE

BLACK BIRD BOOKSTORE

Map 6; 4033 Judah Street, Outer Sunset; ///human.shows.host;
www.blackbirdbooksf.com

Kathryn Grantham founded legendary Lower East Side feminist collective bookstore Bluestockings before swapping Manhattan for San Francisco. In her small Sunset spot, every title is hand-picked and displayed with their covers facing out. It's all about quality over quantity, and allowing stories from diverse voices to stand out.

BOOKSMITH

Map 2; 1644 Haight Street, Haight-Ashbury;
///cups.shot.mixer; www.booksmith.com

This vibrant, roomy independent bookstore stocks both bestsellers and hard-to-find titles. It's also known for bringing in renowned writers for live readings and to host book clubs. Not sure what to read next? Opt for the Dealer's Choice mystery box of books.

OMNIVORE BOOKS ON FOOD

Map 4; 3885 Cesar Chavez Street, Noe Valley; ///keen.ended.crew;
www.omnivorebooks.myshopify.com

Of course San Francisco has an entire store devoted to volumes on food. Located in residential Noe Valley, this cute cornershop is all tall, white bookcases crammed with cookbooks, signed and vintage editions, and obscure food magazines. Check out the free in-store author and chef events, too, where speakers expound on anything from cooking with beans, to how to "drink French."

Vintage Gems

San Franciscans loves vintage – old-school and new-school locals alike. And for every pricey designer resale boutique, there's also a cute neighborhood thrift fair selling one-of-a-kind pieces.

OUT OF THE CLOSET

Map 1; 1498 Polk Street, Polk Gulch; ///given.seats.legal; www.outofthecloset.org

The rails at the wonderfully named Out of the Closet are stuffed to the max with a mix of high street and vintage pieces, as well as some more "fancy dress" items. So people come in to find something for an upcoming costume party, and leave with new favorite Friday-night threads. Better still, 96 cents out of every dollar spent goes to the AIDS Healthcare Foundation.

COMMUNITY THRIFT

Map 4; 623 Valencia Street, The Mission; ///mint.digs.left; www.communitythriftsf.org

You can't miss this huge, hot-pink warehouse, a Mission mainstay since 1982. Locals love rifling through the chaotic assortment of clothes, books, art, and furniture, and feeling good that proceeds go to nearby communities in need. Those who donate their goods get to pick which Bay Area charities benefit from the sale of their items, and it's then listed on the sales receipt – soak up that pay-it-forward glow.

» **Don't leave without** poking your head down Clarion Alley, right next door, which features some of the best murals in the Mission.

MOLTE COSE & BELLE COSE
Map 1; 2036 and 2044 Polk Street, Russian Hill;
///curvy.area.plug; www.moltecose.com

Vintage enthusiasts and self-confessed hipsters rave about these interconnected menswear and womenswear stores. Thoughtfully curated collections feature printed shirts and dresses, plus new pieces from contemporary, vintage-style brands like Voodoo Vixen and 7 Diamonds. Both shops have an inviting, cabinet-of-curiosities feel, with retro dinnerware, cameras, and cocktail sets also filling the shelves. You won't leave empty-handed, trust us.

ALEMANY FLEA MARKET
Map 6; 100 Alemany Boulevard, Bernal Heights; ///follow.nasal.rack;
www.sfgov.org/realestate/alemany-flea-markets

Join families and friends at this ramshackle Sunday market to shop for vintage clothing, furniture, and homeware, or simply for a day out. The vendors, however, are subject to a set of strict rules – if an item is new, it must be 100 percent handmade. Street parking is ample around the area, but try to bring cash as most vendors don't accept credit or debit card transactions.

INNER SUNSET FLEA

Map 5; 800 Irving Street, Inner Sunset; ///copy.anyway.soil; www.isflea.com

There's an old-school community vibe at this popular market, which is set up on Irving Street every second Sunday of the month (April to November). Expect around 30 stalls, with vintage dealers and local makers, and a crowd that's equal parts baseball-cap-wearing retirees and pink-haired hipsters. There's even the odd throwback event, like a pie-baking contest, plus street eats from neighborhood purveyors.

» Don't leave without eating one of Chalos's empanadas or a gluten-free cheesecake cupcake from Shastas Specialized Treats.

RELOVE

Map 1; 1815 Polk Street, Nob Hill; ///train.bunk.taking;
www.shoprelove.com

After something special? You'll love ReLove. A cut above your average vintage store, billing itself as a "resale boutique," this Black-owned treasure trove is an expertly curated assembly of

If you're into antiques, don't miss the Alameda Antiques Faire, held on Alameda Island the first Sunday of each month. There are more than 800 booths of loot to rummage through here, while you soak up the SF skyline views. The ferry ride is just 20 minutes and 100 percent worth it.

niche labels and cult designers, with prices set to keep things as accessible as possible. Check out its Instagram feed to see how the enviably cool staff style newly arrived stock, like Japanese bomber jackets and Gucci hoodies.

THE WASTELAND

Map 2; 1660 Haight Street, Haight-Ashbury; ///purple.native.gangs; www.shopwasteland.com;

In keeping with the neighborhood's rock 'n' roll vibe, this large, airy thrift store specializes in vintage motorcyle jackets, Levi's, and band tees. Alongside these items, the rails also sport a mixture of collectible vintage and high-end designers: think varsity jackets, Chanel espadrilles, and hard-to-find Alexander Wang. Be warned: this isn't exactly your typical dusty thrift store stock, and the prices reflect the fact that it's featured in the likes of *Vogue* and *Nylon*.

RELIC VINTAGE

Map 2; 1605 Haight Street, Haight-Ashbury; ///again.polite.galaxy; www.relicvintagesf.com

One of San Francisco's most idiosyncratic clothing boutiques, Relic Vintage nods to the eccentric styles of the 1920s through to the 1960s. The left-of-center retailer sells vintage clothing and accessories that you'll have a ball rifling through, especially if owner Oran Scott is on hand. Want to feel civilized at home? There are some fabulous 1950s smoking jackets. Costume party on the horizon? Why not try a Marilyn-style dress? You'll part with your paycheck very quickly.

*Before the 90s dot-com boom, **Valencia Street** was seriously avant-garde; its stores targeted women, artists, and the LGBTQ+ community.*

VALENCIA STREET

18TH STREET

GUERRERO STREET

DOLORES STREET

19TH STREET

Indulge at
DANDELION CHOCOLATE

Taste the samples and sip a transcendent frozen hot chocolate at this bean-to-bar chocolate factory.

MISSION

MISSION STREET

Hunt for treasure in
826 VALENCIA PIRATE SUPPLY STORE

Bag a book, board game, or – er – eyepatch at this nonprofit gift shop that helps under-resourced kids develop their literacy.

20TH STREET

VALENCIA STREET

Pop into
TIGERLILY PERFUMERY

Try on Bay Area-made and all-natural fragrances at this shrine to independent scents.

__Señor Sisig__, one of the Mission's favorite food trucks, has been enticing hungry shoppers with its Filipino fare since the noughties.

Update your closet at
GRAVEL & GOLD

Discover your new favorite outfit (or maybe just some socks) at this cool, women-owned design collective.

22ND STREET

0 meters   200
0 yards   200

An afternoon of
indie shopping

SF is famous for its commercial and financial ventures but – when it comes to parting with their hard-earned paychecks – San Franciscans like to shop small and local. And nowhere makes that easier than the Valencia Corridor in the Mission. This 2-mile (3-km) stretch between Duboce Avenue and 26th Street is lined instead by indie crafters, locally designed fashion brands, and small-batch chocolatiers. Perfect for stocking up on treats to take home.

1. Dandelion Chocolate
740 Valencia Street, The Mission; www.dandelion chocolate.com
///fats.shade.rigid

2. 826 Valencia Pirate Supply Store
826 Valencia Street, The Mission; www.826valencia.org
///clean.copper.brains

3. Tigerlily Perfumery
973 Valencia Street, The Mission; www.tigerlily perfumery.com
///sits.noises.afford

4. Gravel & Gold
3266 21st Street, The Mission; www. gravelandgold.com
///junior.search.weeks

📍 **Señor Sisig** ///member.score.owls

18TH STREET

19TH STREET

20TH STREET

21ST STREET

ARTS & CULTURE

San Francisco swells with culture and creativity. Cavernous museums tell the diverse stories of the past, while theater and public art comment on the present and future.

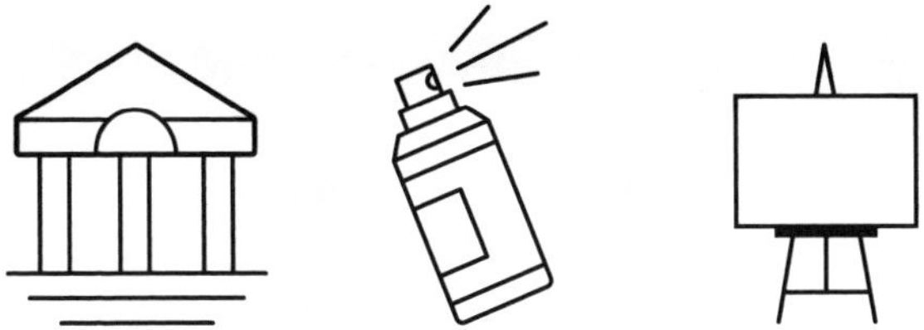

Favorite Museums

Think of a museum and a dusty, fusty institution may come to mind. Not so in San Francisco. Here, science is spiced up with drinks and DJ sets, and collections cover everything from arcade games to vibrators.

GLBT HISTORICAL SOCIETY MUSEUM

**Map 2; 4127 18th Street, The Castro; ///gears.tips.awake;
www.glbthistory.org**

This museum may be small, but it always has something engrossing going on. Rotating exhibitions explore varied subjects, like the third-gender role in Native American communities and queer nightclub photography, while the regular evening panel talks dig into fascinating facets of LGBTQ+ culture. Past topics include the popularity of *The Wizard of Oz* among Anglo-American gay males, and the transgender aesthetic in the movies of Lana and Lilly Wachowski.

SFMOMA

Map 3; 151 3rd Street, SoMa; ///pipe.basis.email; www.sfmoma.org

Folks like to say California doesn't really do high culture, but SFMOMA's teeming galleries are a thorough rebuttal of that. College students, old-timers, and everyone in between pack out

The visiting shows are expensive, but SFMOMA's first two floors are free to access and filled with great contemporary works. | blockbuster visiting exhibitions on high-profile artists. The regular events are also big draws: screenings, offbeat seminars, and the odd party with DJs, real-time art-making, and live music.

EXPLORATORIUM

Map 1; Pier 15, Embarcadero; ///slips.origin.means; www.exploratorium.edu

By day, this hands-on science museum is bursting with sticky swarms of kids. But on After-Dark Thursdays, it's the grown-ups' turn to play. Come 6pm, pop-up bars start serving cocktails, and adults-only talks and demos explore a weekly theme – such as "Sexplorations," which featured a sea urchin "live sex show" and assorted species' testicles.

>> Don't leave without screaming your way around the Tactile Dome, an assault course tackled in the pitch-dark.

SAN FRANCISCO CABLE CAR MUSEUM

Map 1; 1201 Mason Street, Nob Hill; ///badly.dragon.form; www.cablecarmuseum.org

For many San Franciscans, the workings of their cable-car system are a mystery. Which is why they're as delighted as visitors by this little gem. The museum is, in fact, a working powerhouse for the network, where huge wheels pull the cables that run underneath the streets. Wait, what? Yes, it's true: the cars are pulled along by actual underground cables. Still confused? Exactly: that's why you've got to check it out.

MUSÉE MÉCANIQUE

Map 1; Pier 45, Fisherman's Wharf; ///dish.middle.bumpy;
www.museemecanique.com

Most residents steer clear of Fisherman's Wharf. But when family and friends are in town, no one can resist taking them to this oddball arcade. Playable, turn-of-the-century slot machines give insight into the macabre entertainments of our forefolk: there's more than one "game" involving a mechanical execution. Weird, hilarious, and sort of educational, it's the most fun you can have in a room of antiques.

CALIFORNIA ACADEMY OF SCIENCES

Map 5; 55 Music Concourse Drive, Golden Gate Park;
///axed.latest.smiles; www.calacademy.org

Does any other city in the world have a museum that offers not just a rainforest dome, a living roof, an aquarium, and a planetarium, but a resident mixologist, too? We think not. Curious 20- and

Feeling peckish after a night of cocktails at the California Academy of Sciences? Head to the nearby Sunset district for dinner at Toyose *(www.sftoyose.wixsite.com/toyose)*. This late-night Korean restaurant is housed in a garage (yes, a literal garage), where huge sharing plates of spicy wings, seafood pancakes, and kimchi fried rice pair perfectly with cold Korean beers and a fun party atmosphere.

30-somethings head here for monthly NightLife events, where each bar features its own seasonal cocktail from said mixologist. There's also live music, food, panel talks, and activities, which range across everything from print-making to brewing beer.

MUSEUM OF THE AFRICAN DIASPORA

Map 3; 685 Mission Street, SoMa; ///video.script.attend; www.moadsf.org

Check out this art museum during one of the Yerba Buena district's Third Thursday events, when there's free entry, food and drink, and a mixed crowd to mingle with. Art, music, and spoken-word shows focus solely on work by and about African diasporas. At other times, there are film screenings, poetry readings, and artists' talks.

» Don't leave without swinging into the neaby Yerba Buena Center for the Arts, another Third Thursday venue just across the street.

GOOD VIBRATIONS

Map 1; 1620 Polk Street, Nob Hill; ///cheek.dwell.smiled; www.antiquevibratormuseum.com

Good Vibrations isn't exactly a family-friendly venue— but it's absolutely a left-of-center treat for the adult crowd. An antique vibrator museum, it's a "Historical Sexual Treasure" that chronicles how female autonomy and sexual identity have overlapped with the evolution and normalization of sex toys in society. Museum goers who want to spice up their private life can peruse a wide array of self-pleasuring devices post-tour, available to purchase and take home as an intimate souvenir.

City History

Folks 'round these parts are proud of their city's history, with an eclectic bunch of nonprofits and indie institutes dedicated to local trailblazers, as well as immigrant and other marginalized communities.

THE BEAT MUSEUM

Map 1; 540 Broadway, North Beach; ///turns.desk.patio; www.kerouac.com

The events agenda at this diminutive indie spot keeps the spirit of the Beat Generation alive and kicking. Bohemians gather for feminist readings, small-press launch parties, and the occasional vigil for departed Beat-scene heroes. It's San Francisco as it used to be: disheveled literary types kicking against the system with novels and poems, ideas, and debate. There's also a little movie theater that shows Beat-era films.

HAIGHT-ASHBURY CLOCK

Map 2; 1500 Haight Street, Haight-Ashbury; ///lime.slate.first

At the corner where Haight and Ashbury streets meet, pilgrimaging hippies pay their respects by raising their eyes to this clock. It's permanently stuck at 4:20, the international sign for "time to smoke marijuana" – apt, given that Haight-Ashbury was the epicenter of the Summer of Love in 1967. Nearby trinket stores cash in, selling tie-dye and incense sticks, but you can still find some real hippies settled into the sofas at next-door's Coffee to the People, drinking fair-trade blends like "Global Karma" and "Bohemian Decaf."

» **Don't leave without** seeing the "Grateful Dead House," a block away at 710 Ashbury Street. This purple Victorian town house was the band's crash-pad during 1967's revolutionary summer.

CHINESE HISTORICAL SOCIETY OF AMERICA MUSEUM

Map 1; 965 Clay Street, Chinatown; ///cult.sage.listed; www.chsa.org

San Francisco's Chinatown is one of the oldest in the country, and it remains a buzzing hub for the city's Chinese-American community today. This small but brilliantly curated museum honors both the district's present and its past, with rotating exhibits, art shows, and an events calendar of panel discussions and "documentary watch parties" exploring the Chinese immigrant experience in the US.

Try it!
WALKING TOUR

For an insight into Chinatown the community – rather than Chinatown the tourist trap – check out one of the small group walks led by Chinatown Alleyway Tours *(www.chinatownalleywaytours.org)*.

ANGEL ISLAND IMMIGRATION STATION

Map 6; Angel Island State Park; ///runner.oldest.sunset; www.aiisf.org

Most visitors head to Angel Island for a hike and a picnic. But locals know its darker legacy as the "Ellis Island of the West," where many immigrants arriving via the Pacific were held in detention. The station today remembers their experiences with a series of oral histories. Spot the Chinese poetry carved into the walls of the barracks.

RAINBOW HONOR WALK

Map 2; Corner of 19th Street and Collingwood Street, The Castro; ///mats.minus.spring; www.rainbowhonorwalk.org

Stretching along the Castro's main drag, this LGBTQ+ "Walk of Fame" honors the neighborhood's long history of queer activism. Bronze plaques commemorate pioneers like James Baldwin and Gertrude Stein, who would no doubt be tickled by the cheeky shopfronts that accompany the route: The Sausage Factory restaurant, Hand Job nail salon, and Knobs men's clothing store.

» **Don't leave without** snapping a pic of your feet on the Castro's rainbow crosswalks. If you don't, were you ever really there?

ST. JOHN COLTRANE CHURCH

Map 5; 2097 Turk Boulevard, NoPa; ///drive.hunter.unique; www.coltranechurch.org

Inside this boxy yellow church, the core congregation will often be joined by a couple of jazz buffs and a curious tourist. That's because this is no ordinary place of worship: its patron saint is legendary

A popular "guided sound meditation" to Coltrane's album *A Love Supreme* is held on the first Sunday of every month.

saxophonist John Coltrane. Locals Franzo and Marina King founded this one-off in the 1960s, and it was later invited into the African Orthodox Church. Services, which may include jazz jams, are open to all.

RINCON CENTER MURALS

Map 1; 121 Spear Street, Embarcadero; ///mental.fats.lowest

The 24-hour lobby of a property management company might not strike you as an obvious place to find a slice of city history. Once inside, however, you'll find the controversial 1940s murals of Anton Refregier, who was commissioned to paint the history of San Francisco in this former Post Office. His too-honest portraits – riots, strikes, and the Depression – led to calls to remove the "Communist" works. But, against all odds, they were preserved.

TENDERLOIN MUSEUM

Map 3; 398 Eddy Street, Tenderloin; ///simply.awake.lights;
www.tenderloinmuseum.org

The event program at this gutsy nonprofit tempts a sophisticated crowd to the Tenderloin, a district best known for drug problems and homeless encampments. An evening calendar of documentary films, play readings, and archive photo shows tells a different side to the story, revealing the neighborhood's historic role in some of San Francisco's most progressive movements and explaining why making the district visible, and city officials accountable, is vital.

Public Art

Far from being just another photo opportunity, public art in San Francisco is a long-held tradition. The city is embroidered with characteristically creative pieces that tell stories about its community and landscape.

LANGUAGE OF THE BIRDS

Map 1; 320 Columbus Avenue, North Beach; ///reward.souk.garage

Come see this permanent piece at night, when embedded LED lights – powered by solar, of course – flash alternatively trippy and soothing patterns across the work. Representing the intersection of North Beach's Italian, Chinese, and beatnik cultures, a flock of books, resembling paper cranes, are suspended in flight. Watch the light show from the west side of Columbus, then move in for a closer look at the phrases embedded in the street beneath.

ANDY GOLDSWORTHY SCULPTURES

Map 5; Main Post, Presidio National Park; ///blank.ridge.unrealistic; www.presidio.gov/art

The 3-mile (5-km) hiking loop around these site-specific pieces in the Presidio is about as San Francisco as it gets. Ancient, urban forest; free, nature-hewn art; and weekend walkers in their finest athleisure gear: you couldn't be anywhere else. Start at *Tree Fall*, an enormous branch exploding into the Main Post building, and stroll counterclockwise until you get to *Wood Line*, in a eucalyptus grove.

» **Don't leave without** treating yourself to a pastry at award-winning B. Patisserie, just a few blocks from Wood Line, in Pacific Heights.

SEA CHANGE KINETIC SCULPTURE
Map 3; Pier 40, Embarcadero; ///cafe.pillow.school

Mark di Suvero's enormous scrap-metal sculptures are renowned across the world – so San Franciscans are especially smug about having their very own on the bayfront. Standing 70 ft (21 m) tall by Pier 40, this bright-orange abstract giant has a circular steel top that moves with the wind. Its location has particular resonance for di Suvero: born to Italian parents in Shanghai, he moved to the City by the Bay in 1942 and Pier 40 was his first port of entry.

GRACE CATHEDRAL
Map 1; 1100 California Street, Nob Hill; ///toned.likes.rainy; www.gracecathedral.org

Likely the funkiest cathedral of all time, this Gothic masterpiece atop swanky Nob Hill has an artist-in-residence program. New pieces are installed and performed on a regular basis, so on any given visit you might see LED sculptures, installations hanging from the ceiling, or perhaps live ballet pieces. The progressive minds behind Grace say they're "reimagining the church" to inspire joy and wonder regardless of religion.

MISSION MURALS

Map 4; Balmy Alley, The Mission; ///blind.notes.prove;
www.precitaeyes.org

The colorful protest murals daubed across the Mission's buildings and alleyways aren't just great art – they're essential to understanding the district. The neighborhood's talented Latin-American muralists paint about where they've come from and the challenges they face in San Francisco: Balmy Alley alone has memorable pieces about the Salvadoran civil war and ongoing gentrification. New works are being added all the time, so trips to hot spots such as Clarion Alley are rarely the same twice.

» **Don't leave without** admiring the Women's Building on 18th Street. Its five-story exterior is covered in murals of powerful females, from a Puerto Rican revolutionary to a Palestinian peacekeeper.

PEEPHOLE CINEMA

Map 4; 280 Orange Alley, The Mission; ///tested.hooks.salt;
www.peepholecinema.com

Generally, we don't recommend peeping into other people's houses. But looking through the hole in the red side-wall down Orange Alley – identifiable by a discreet hanging sign – is strongly encouraged. Peer in and you'll see a stream of short, silent movies, curated around a theme; past series have explored the supernatural in urban environments, futuristic animations of loss, and visual illusions. It's worth following Peephole's Twitter for updates: sometimes there are even opportunities to meet the artists behind the movies for drinks.

Liked by the locals

"My favorite mural is a community painting, created by Mission youth alongside local artists Max Marttila and Fred Alvarado. At the corner of 25th Street and York, it's a collection of Latin legends like Mala Rodriguez, celebrating the district's rich musical traditions."

PATRICIA ROSE, TOUR GUIDE FOR
PRECITA EYES MURAL TOURS

Top Theaters

San Francisco doesn't have the dazzling array of big shows you find in New York or London. But it does have a great bunch of grassroots theaters staging experimental plays and telling diverse stories.

AMERICAN CONSERVATORY THEATER

Map 1; 415 Geary Street, Union Square;
///reds.armed.detail; www.act-sf.org

The ACT embodies the San Francisco tradition of reinvention, with a program that leans into rethinking classics. That could mean refocusing Caryl Churchill's feminist play *Top Girls* through the lens of working-class women of color, or a stage dramatization of Khaled Hosseini's critically acclaimed novel *A Thousand Splendid Suns*. Many end up winning Tonys and/or going on national tour.

SF MASONIC

Map 1; 1111 California Street, Nob Hill;
///master.fits.model; www.sfmasonic.com

There's something very San Franciscan about catching live podcast recordings and blockbuster comedy headliners inside an extravagant Masonic temple at the top of Nob Hill. The building is unmissable: a mid-century modern monolith of mosaic windows, 12-ft- (4-m-) high statues, and grand, symbolic friezes. Be sure to check out the massive mural in the lobby, too. It's made from seashells, grass, stones, and the soil of every county in the state.

» Don't leave without sipping a wind-down wine at Nob Hill Cafe, a relaxed, old-school local spot a couple of blocks north.

THE MARSH

Map 4; 1062 Valencia Street, The Mission; ///tonic.crisp.vibrate; www.themarsh.org

There are just 100 seats at this intimate indie theater, which is all about showcasing locally written and produced plays. There's a lot of one-person-show stuff, featuring a diverse pool of actors and often focusing on personal experiences (past pieces include *Black Virgins Are Not For Hipsters*, a spoof of local tech culture, and *The O Diary*, about one woman's quest to make friends with her orgasm). There are also dance pieces and original musicals.

PlayGround, a Bay Area playwright incubator, often puts on pay-what-you-can previews of new works at its Potrero Stage theater in Potrero Hill *(www.potrerostage.org)*. It's a great way to see local works-in-progress at a discounted price, and you might even discover a rising star – several of PlayGround's alumni have gone on to win awards.

CURRAN

Map 1; 445 Geary Street, Union Square;
///casino.booth.adding; www.sfcurran.com

This brilliant (and beautiful) theater is where you'll catch larger-scale experimental shows, some before they go on to try their luck in NYC. It premiered *Soft Power*, an ambitious (and hilarious) musical showing the US through a Chinese lens, which went on to be an Off-Broadway hit; and also staged *The Jungle*, turning the venue into the famous migrant camp in Calais.

NEW CONSERVATORY THEATRE CENTER

Map 3; 25 Van Ness Avenue, Noe Valley;
///intend.exam.boxing; www.nctcsf.org

Known for queer storytelling with a universal appeal, this small drama house promotes inclusivity and acceptance, all the while instilling audience members with a sense that they're not alone – no matter what plight they're facing. It's a theater house that's as inviting and warm as it is eye-opening and socially engaging.

SAN FRANCISCO PLAYHOUSE

Map 1; 2nd Floor, 450 Post Street, Union Square;
///powder.goad.hammer; www.sfplayhouse.org

There's a very Off-Broadway spirit at this small nonprofit on the second floor of the Kensington Park Hotel. SF's theater fans come here to get their fix of fresh works: the in-house New Play Program has developed a number of pieces that went on to receive national acclaim. You can also catch plays in development at the Monthly Reading Series, where works-in-progress are performed without the accoutrements of costumes or full sets.

THEATRE OF YUGEN
Map 4; 2840 Mariposa Street, The Mission; ///resort.shield.hours; www.theatreofyugen.org

This experimental troupe has been bringing its works to the San Francisco stage for more than 30 years, but only recently found itself a permanent space in the Mission. Original pieces at the teeny nonprofit theater explore Japanese performance styles of *noh* (drama) and *kyogen* (satire), often using them to tell modern American stories: an Edgar Allen Poe puppet show, perhaps, or a meditation on the Native American experience.

LORRAINE HANSBERRY THEATER
Map 2; 762 Fulton Street, Fillmore; ///wings.juror.guilty; www.lhtsf.org

Located inside Fillmore's African American Art & Culture Complex, this not-for-profit theater company stages plays exclusively by and about people of color, covering everything from the African American canon to new and boundary-pushing works. A particular focus on female playwrights also brings modern classics like *Single Black Female* to a diverse crowd from all over the bay – pieces always play to a packed house.

» Don't leave without seeing the famous "Painted Ladies," a row of Victorian houses two blocks west at Alamo Square Park.

Indie Galleries

As rents have rocketed, the city's art scene has been forced out to the fringes. Ever-inventive, local creatives have carved out art spaces wherever they can – seeking them out is an adventure that reaps rewards.

SOMARTS CULTURAL CENTER

Map 3; 934 Brannan Street, SoMa; ///inches.bind.heads; www.somarts.org

You can't miss this bright-red building, right by the freeway. No, the postindustrial exterior isn't pretty, but the multidisciplinary space inside more than makes up for it. Leaning on SoMa's inclusive legacy, shows here favor work by people historically marginalized by the art world. Think video, performance, and installation pieces from artists with disabilities, and queer and immigrant movements.

Try it!
FIGURE DRAWING

Want to create your own masterpiece? SoMa runs figure drawing classes on Saturdays for just $8. Run by an expert, the classes will really help you practice your form and expression. Perfect third-date activity.

ET AL.

Map 1; 620 Kearny Street, Chinatown; ///opera.vibe.duck; www.etaletc.com

In the basement of a Chinatown laundromat, this quite literally underground gallery makes space for experimental art. The founders wanted to find a way to show local work that didn't fit into a prescribed category, and so decided to do it themselves, in between their day jobs. The obscure result is delightfully unpredictable.

» Don't leave without hydrating at Steap Tea Bar, a block west. The green tea with mascarpone foam topping is a standout.

AFRICAN AMERICAN ART & CULTURE COMPLEX

Map 2; 762 Fulton Street, Fillmore; ///wings.juror.guilty; www.aaacc.org

Preserving the rich Black heritage of Fillmore is no easy task, given the relentless gentrification that has chased many longtime residents out. The AAACC, then, is a must-visit: a one-stop shop for art shows, film screenings, and literary panels that focus on works by people of color.

CREATIVITY EXPLORED

Map 4; 3245 16th Street, The Mission; ///ships.zooms.family; www.creativityexplored.com

Art really can change lives. Take Creativity Explored, which acts as a springboard for artists with developmental disabilities to showcase their work and earn money through their talent. And, unlike a lot of art spaces, the gallery itself is a genuinely welcoming place to look and buy a piece. If you don't make a purchase, consider leaving a donation.

LUGGAGE STORE GALLERY

Map 3; 1007 Market Street, Mid-Market; ///flags.washed.simple;
www.luggagestoregallery.org

It's little wonder this place is only frequented by those in-the-know. Stuffed between the emblems of old and new Mid-Market – on one side panhandlers and, on the other, a brand-new Yotel robot hotel – the Luggage Store Gallery looks like a derelict building. The only sign there might be something more than meets the eye here is a strip of well-tended plants growing out of the facade. See that crummy door plastered with stickers? Yes, that's the entrance. Upstairs, though, you'll find an eclectic collection of street art by Bay Area up-and-comers, who this gallery does great work to support.

>> Don't leave without visiting the nearby "Tenderloin National Forest," a previously squalid Tenderloin alley that was transformed by the gallery owners into a green space for art and performance.

CATHARINE CLARK GALLERY

Map 3; 248 Utah Street, Potrero Hill; ///quench.lately.crisis;
www.cclarkgallery.com

The Catharine Clark Gallery is one of those places you can always rely on to be exhibiting a headline-generating piece. You know, like an interactive show where you're encouraged to spy on other gallery-goers, or a White House built entirely from bullets. New exhibits open every six weeks, ensuring constant fodder for debates with your friends no matter how often you visit. And you can be sure that, whatever you see, you'll still be talking about it on the long journey home from Potrero Hill.

Liked by the locals

"In the midst of the nation's biggest wealth gap, the Bay Area art scene is on the cutting edge of politics, social change, and innovation of form. Hence why San Francisco continues to bring forward the most transformative artists of our times."

DARRYL SMITH, CO-DIRECTOR OF
THE LUGGAGE STORE GALLERY

This dead-end street was transformed into an arts hub in 2016. **Dogpatch Arts Plaza** *is painted with urban art and hosts live music.*

④ Admire the view from THE RAMP

Stop for a restorative sip at this local secret: a charismatically rickety, outdoor waterfront bar with happy hour specials.

Crane Cove Park

3RD STREET

STREET

19TH STREET

Esprit Park

DOGPATCH

It's thought that the area's name comes from the American comic strip Li'l Abner, *which is set in a place called* **Dogpatch**.

20TH STREET

ILLINOIS STREET

Chow down at JUST FOR YOU

Refuel with a fresh-squeezed lemonade and sandwich, made from homebaked bread, at this local favorite, which is lined with vintage travel and theater posters.

② 22ND STREET

③ Mooch around the MUSEUM OF CRAFT AND DESIGN

Peruse works by painters, sculptors, and technologists at the MCD before swinging by the shop (where you'll want to buy everything in sight).

MINNESOTA STREET

3RD STREET

STREET

23RD STREET

① Begin at MINNESOTA STREET PROJECT

Kick-start your afternoon by spending a couple of hours browsing the 13 indie galleries inside this warehouse complex.

0 meters 250
0 yards 250

25TH STREET

An afternoon in
arty Dogpatch

You won't spot many tourists in this dockside neighborhood, a decidedly unphotogenic part of town squished between an industrial port and a freeway. But looks aren't everything and with rents still on the affordable side Dogpatch has fast become the city's newest and most exciting creative hub. Here, warehouses once busy with shipbuilding and repairs are now jammed with galleries and design collectives. This afternoon amble takes you through the best of Dogpatch's arts scene within just a few short blocks.

San Francisco Bay

1. Minnesota Street Project
1275 Minnesota Street, Dogpatch; www.minnesotastreetproject.com
///mostly.drank.motor

2. Just For You
732 22nd Street, Dogpatch; www.justforyoucafe.com
///caller.cover.vast

3. Museum of Craft and Design
2569 3rd Street, Dogpatch; www.sfmcd.org
///wiped.desire.cove

4. The Ramp
855 Terry A. Francois Boulevard, Dogpatch; www.rampsf.com
///hardly.deep.pints

Dogpatch Arts Plaza ///verge.meals.rift

NIGHTLIFE

Anything goes when it comes to a night out in SF. From sedate spoken-word performances to raucous LGBTQ+ shows, the city's nightlife is all about self-expression.

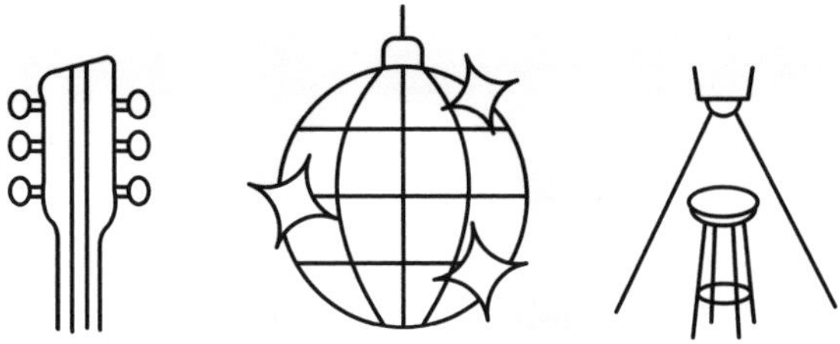

Live Music

This city has always embraced boundary-pushing music, from the Fillmore jazz days to the Grateful Dead's era-defining rock. Its independent venues still play by those principles, favoring up-and-coming acts.

RICKSHAW STOP

Map 3; 155 Fell Street, Hayes Valley; ///surely.memory.tuned; www.rickshawstop.com

A grungy little venue in an old auto repair shop, Rickshaw Stop is a San Francisco institution. Expect experimental, avant-garde, and indie acts. It's super-busy and more than a little rowdy, but the cool kids know to get here early and head for the top floor to snag a seat.

THE INDEPENDENT

Map 2; 628 Divisadero Street, NoPa; ///brave.gossip.wheels; www.theindependentsf.com

This intimate venue is the kind of spot bands love to play at, even if they could fill a larger stage. Modern icons have performed here but the organizers also have an eye for booking acts just before they blow up: MIA and The xx both made appearances prior to getting big. It's pretty much standing room only but there's always space to dance.

THE FILLMORE

Map 2; 1805 Geary Boulevard, Fillmore; ///sling.plus.stared; thefillmore.com

If you're on the hunt for a slice of the city's music history, head to this iconic concert hall. It's got a knack for hosting the most decade-defining acts (Tina Turner and Jimi Hendrix are among the alumni). A grand rep also means a grand venue: think red velvet drapes and chandeliers.

THE CHAPEL

Map 4; 777 Valencia Street, The Mission;
///copper.trail.search; www.thechapelsf.com

Follow the young crowd to this converted church on any given night and you may just find your new favorite band. You could catch Afro-Chicano beats, Irish folk-pop, or even a punk legend. The vaulted ceiling produces unique acoustics, and the atmosphere is just as special; be prepared to get cosy with the locals – it can get pretty jammed.

BLACK CAT

Map 3; 400 Eddy Street, Tenderloin; ///cities.grapes.alone;
www.blackcatsf.com

There's a very in-the-know feel to this sleek jazz club. Most people swerve gritty Eddy Street unless they know what lies behind 400's brick facade. Jazz heads come to see cool combos play the basement stage (more young bassists in beanies than grizzled old dudes). Dine at a front table, or slide into a velvet booth if you're just here for the jazz.

» Don't leave without sipping a Tenderloin Manhattan, which packs an even bigger punch than the cocktail it's based on.

Solo, Pair, Crowd

Fancy a boogie? Have a date to impress with your tuneful tastes? It's your bithday? San Francisco has a music mecca for every occasion.

FLYING SOLO

Catch some cool cats

SFJAZZ, in Hayes Valley, is a 100-seat, glass-and-concrete auditorium purpose-built for live jazz shows. Greats from all over the world often grace its main stage.

IN A PAIR

Heart and soul

Get down on date night with a trip to Union Square's basement spot Biscuits & Blues: a winning combo of live blues bands, classic Southern soul food, and tasty cocktails.

FOR A CROWD

Group singalong

Take a support team to The Mint Karaoke Lounge, a Hayes Valley mainstay where, instead of private booths, singers perform on a live stage (and are even beamed onto TVs at the bar — we warned you).

# GREAT AMERICAN MUSIC HALL
Map 3; 859 O'Farrell Street, Tenderloin; ///sorters.region.rams;
www.slimspresents.com

Between the dive bars and "gentlemen's clubs" of the upper TL, this
110-year-old venue is a real diamond in the rough. Newbies are always
wowed by its incongruous opulence: the Italianate moldings and
ornate columns form the backdrop for moshpits and rock bands.

SHEBA PIANO LOUNGE
Map 2; 1419 Fillmore Street, Fillmore;
///soils.rotate.globe; www.shebapianolounge.com

Most people stumble upon this spot, then swiftly tell everyone they
know about it. It's a triple threat: amazing Ethiopian food (with spices
shipped from Ethiopia); a living-room-like space; and free live music
(jazz, blues, soul, Latin) every night. After dinner, move to the sofas: the
band starts up around 8:30pm and is always worth staying around for.
» Don't leave without taking advantage of the "red-eye" special,
Sheba's nightly late happy hour (from 10pm until closing).

BOOM BOOM ROOM
Map 2; 1601 Fillmore Street, Fillmore;
///penny.curving.pipe; www.boomboomroom.com

Along with Sheba, this is the only joint keeping the flame of Fillmore's
jazz history burning. It's every inch the down-at-home juke joint: red
walls, checkerboard floor, vinyl booths. A high-energy spot, the crowd
keeps grooving and the live funk, jazz, and blues keep booming 'til 3am.

Cool Clubs

San Franciscans typically prefer a dive bar to a super-club, perhaps because there's no dress code (perfect for a T-shirts and jeans combo), but there are a few late-night dance spots if you know where to look.

CAT CLUB

Map 3; 1190 Folsom Street, SoMa; ///buddy.shade.mull; www.sfcatclub.com

Don't get your days mixed up at this fun, sticky-floored spot: two of its most popular themed nights are "1984" and "Bondage-A-Go-Go." CC's defining characteristics – cheap drinks, no judgment, and great music – attract a low-key bunch who just want to dance. The exposed brick walls, spotlit cages, and leather couches might make it look a bit seedy, but the regular nights are friendly and the vibe is always chill.

MADRONE ART BAR

Map 2; 500 Divisadero Street, NoPa; ///likely.exam.basket; www.madroneartbar.com

Ask any SF stalwart where to head on a Monday and Madrone will be their only answer. The long-running Motown night never gets old, if the masses that pack into the teeny bar are any indication. The bar also doubles as an art gallery, with rotating exhibitions to keep you occupied if there's a lull between the grooveable tunes. The "Prince vs Michael Jackson" dance party, every first Saturday of the month, is also a dearly held tradition. Arrive via an ATM: it's cash only.

THE KNOCKOUT

Map 4; 3223 Mission Street, Bernal Heights; ///banks.hello.slowly; www.theknockoutsf.com

Red walls, leather booths, vintage pinball: The Knockout epitomizes a neighborhood dive bar. Beloved by a young, alternative, and easy-going crew, there's entertainment here every night. During the week it's all about live Bay Area bands, bingo nights, and trivia (including a monthly Simpsons quiz where they serve Duff beer), while on the weekend, the place transforms into a massive dance party, with DJs spinning funk and house bangers.

» Don't leave without snapping a pic in the photo booth, for a reminder of what you looked like when the night wound down at 2am.

TEMPLE

Map 3; 540 Howard Street, SoMa; ///acted.rate.task; www.templesf.com

If international superstar DJs are your thing, you better head to Temple – it's probably the closest SF gets to a "superclub." You'll find two floors with flashing, floor-to-ceiling LED lights that lend a futur-istic feel. Upstairs pumps EDM, while downstairs is R&B and hip-hop. It'll be a big night, but some things you need to know: one, line up for guest-list entry early, or you'll wait an hour; two, it's a notorious spot for people (both men and women) looking for a hookup.

AUDIO

Map 3; 316 11th Street, SoMa; ///blend.cable.cases; www.audiosf.com

This small, laser-lit club has a big reputation thanks to the renowned techno and house DJs headlining on the bill. Audio geeks and DJ wannabes love the Funktion-One sound system, which has a huge impact in a space this size – your ears will be buzzing long after you've left. Keep an eye out for the regular day parties, popular for pairing techno with free pizza. Oh, and a word of advice: watch those stairs down to the sunken dance floor (someone always stumbles).

BUTTER

Map 3; 354 11th Street, SoMa; ///epic.shady.inform;
www.smoothasbutter.com

There are dive bars, and then there's Butter. The ultimate antidote to San Francisco's health-conscious, finely crafted, and trend-forward culture, this novel spot gleefully serves deep-fried Twinkies and "cocktails" mixed with off-brand fruit sodas. The let-your-hair-

Desperate for a late-night snack after a heady night out in SoMa's nightlife district? Head to DNA Pizza (www.dnapizza.com) which is on the same block as both Audio and Butter. These guys are open 'til 4am on weekends (2am during the week) and have a range of veggie and vegan options.

down, dance-like-nobody's-watching energy is helped along handsomely by $3 jello shots and tall-boy beer cans served in brown paper bags. The music matches the anti-cool attitude: 1980s, 1990s, and a heavy-serving of Top 40.

» **Don't leave without** trying one of Butter's "signature cocktails," like the "Butter's Bottle Service" (a pint of beer topped with amaro).

RAVEN BAR

Map 3; 1151 Folsom Street, SoMa; ///pies.mile.swaps; www.ravenbarsf.com

Wannabe B-boys (and some real ones) come to bust a move at this 1990s hip-hop bar. It's no-frills fun, crammed tight with young folks busting moves to match their favorite dance videos, screened in the dance area, and flirting over rounds of shots. Some say the party has outgrown the space – weekends are a sardines situation – but with cheap drinks, and top tunes there's not a lot of room to complain either.

THE ENDUP

Map 3; 401 6th Street, SoMa; ///factories.sleeps.trash; www.theendupsf.com

Look, you don't come to The EndUp because it's a particularly great club. You come because it's the only place in town that keeps going past 4am. Just check the name: all the hardcore revelers who don't want to go home end up here, and things don't really ramp up until after all the other clubs shut down. It's not classy by any stretch of the imagination, but if you're down for a big night, why fight it?

Comedy Nights

The hometown of Robin Williams and rising stars like Ali Wong, SF has a strong comedy history. Audiences can catch the big names, but more interesting are the newbies performing in tiny improv theaters and bars.

PUNCH LINE

Map 1; 444 Battery Street, Jackson Square;
///names.decreased.member; www.punchlinecomedyclub.com

The best comedy spots are teeny tiny. Take Punch Line, a small upstairs spot, where comics perform against a painted backdrop of San Francisco. It's a great place to see an intimate show from the occasional superstar, or superstar-in-waiting. Need proof? Robin Williams started here and there's been a grand tradition of feisty

Try it!
BECOME A COMIC

Always making your loved ones laugh? Put those jokes into practice at SF Comedy College (www.sfcomedycollege.com). It runs a free introductory stand-up class, plus paid classes where you can perfect your set.

female comedians taking the Punch Line stage – a rare claim for stand-up venues. Amy Schumer, Ellen DeGeneres, Chelsea Handler, and Margaret Cho, to name a few, have all performed here.

CHEAPER THAN THERAPY

Map 1; 533 Sutter Street, Union Square; ///spicy.rash.rash; www.cttcomedy.com

This raucous comedy night, founded by Bay Area comedians Jon Allen and Scott Simpson and hosted in the tiny Shelton Theater, always plays to a packed house. From Thursday to Sunday, local comedians perform 15-minute sets in front of a dedicated crowd of comedy fans. In a unique twist, after the show, Jon and Scott invite the audience to go for drinks with the performers. Is it any wonder that people keep coming back again and again?

» **Don't leave without** checking out the rotating fine art exhibitions in the Shelton's bar during a pause in performances.

STAGE WERX

Map 4; 446 Valencia Street, The Mission; ///chest.rope.shado; wwww.stagewerx.org

It's first-come, first-served at this 70-seat space, which hosts free Friday- and Saturday-night improv shows. Friday night's "Your F-ed Up Relationship" is particularly popular: audience members share deets of failed liaisons, which performers then work into the sketch comedy. Past Saturday-night shows have included "The Iron Stage" – a comic retelling of the hit TV series *Game of Thrones*.

COBB'S COMEDY CLUB
Map 1; 915 Columbus Avenue, North Beach; ///goes.brick.chart;
www.cobbscomedy.com

SF's classic and much-loved comedy club has been going since the 1980s and, we'll be honest, it hasn't changed much in the ensuing decades. Luckily, you're not here for the slick aesthetics, but rather the major acts (the likes of Dave Chapelle and Dana Carvey have rocked up in the past). Those on first dates might want to arrive early to nab a seat at the back – performers pick on the front row.

SECRET IMPROV SOCIETY
Map 1; 533 Sutter Street, Theater District; ///global.help.games;
www.secretimprov.com

Comedy and free Oreos? We thought you'd never ask. Head here on a Friday or Saturday night for some quick-thinking physical comedy with the city's unsung talents. Name a scenario and they'll transform it into an energetic performance that will have you snorting wildly. Hold back in the bar after the show and, if you're lucky, one of the performers might swing by to play the piano and have a singsong.

PIANOFIGHT
Map 3; 144 Taylor Street, Tenderloin; ///chin.daily.school;
www.pianofight.com

This indie cabaret bar goes unnoticed by many thanks to its perch in the heart of the Tenderloin. That's a shame, because it's one of the more interesting arts venues in the city, with a mix of stand-up,

Don't stop at comedy. Pianofight has two simple performance spaces, staging short plays and dance shows by local artists.

sketch, and improv comedy on the main stage, plus drag and cabaret shows – all of it local and new. The bar itself is a gem, pulling Bay Area beers and mixing a boggling array of house cocktails.

THE SETUP

Map 3; 222 Hyde Street, Tenderloin; ///vows.salt.homes; www.setupcomedy.com

It doesn't get more intimate than The Setup, a weekly comedy night in a tiny Tenderloin basement where you'll be sitting just feet from the comedians. Yes, it's an overused phrase, but this place really is a "hidden gem." The Saturday-night show is just 90 minutes, but it's ram-packed with laughs thanks to a lineup of five to six local comics.

» Don't leave without appreciating that this basement was once the green room at the legendary Black Hawk jazz club, played by all the greats (think Miles Davis, Billie Holiday, and Thelonius Monk).

BEST OF SAN FRANCISCO STAND-UP COMEDY

Map 1; 582 Market Street, Financial District; ///admire.sound.waters; www.bestofsfstandup.com

Flashier than many of its counterparts, this show is based in a plush theater in the swanky Hobart Building. Starring bigger names from the likes of NBC, HBO, and Comedy Central, the Friday-night lineup is especially popular with out-of-towners looking for big laughs.

Movie Theaters

This is a city that loves arthouse, but also embraces late-night horror marathons, themed showings, and throwback classics. Whichever local cinema you walk into, you're sure to find an eclectic mix of screenings.

ROXIE THEATER

Map 4; 3117 16th Street, The Mission; ///lives.trader.farmer;
www.roxie.com

Movie buffs and arty types love this nonprofit arthouse cinema, a historic Art Deco beauty with a penchant for documentaries and foreign indies. Part of the joy of visiting this century-old art hub is the thought that generations of San Franciscans have been coming here – showcasing their own short films, debating political pieces, and praising the city's finest documentary makers.

BALBOA THEATER

Map 6; 3630 Balboa Street, Outer Richmond; ///jazzy.equal.hurry;
www.cinemasf.com

This vintage 1920s theater is a local favorite among the outer reaches of Richmond, with its nostalgic vibes and proper butter popcorn. The small screen here shows the occasional new release in a schedule

Don't walk too quickly past Balboa's foyer or you'll miss the old-school arcade game collection – Donkey Kong is a favorite.

packed with indies, documentaries, monthly underground horror specials (sample titles: *The Slime People*; *Satan's Cheerleaders*), and screenings with expert commentaries and filmmaker panels.

CASTRO THEATRE

Map 2; 429 Castro Street, The Castro;
///copy.pushy.frock; www.castrotheatre.com

Catching a flick at this opulent city landmark feels like a throwback to the moviegoing golden era. Buy your tickets at the box office out front, then head inside for a double feature. The in-house organ player kicks things off by keying classic tunes on the Wurlitzer before the curtain goes up. Along with themed screenings, there are regular drag extravaganzas from the queen of the local scene, Peaches Christ.

» Don't leave without looking up! The Castro has the last known leatherette (a historic, leather imitation design) ceiling in the United States.

AMC METREON 16

Map 3; 135 4th Street #3000, SoMa; ///served.agree.tooth;
www.amctheatres.com

AMC is known for its nostalgia and its lengthy library of feature films. This is a huge, multilevel branch of the movie-theater company, smack-dab in the middle of shopping outlets, showing most of the current big-hitters. Matinee screenings are quite cheap, attracting families and students, if you're looking for some budget entertainment.

OTHER CINEMA

Map 4; 992 Valencia Street, The Mission; ///tags.lime.mixer;
www.othercinema.com

This snug cinema is as avant-garde as they come – and bear in mind San Francisco is the West Coast's bastion of the avant-garde. Set up by Craig Baldwin, a homegrown experimental filmmaker, Other Cinema curates radical and unorthodox local movies; televised series of yesteryears are at times given a big-screen treatment. It's garnered a niche, but loyal, following, quickly becoming a community hub for independent filmmakers and multimedia artists (who often show their films here and stick around for an engaging talk with the audience).

ALAMO DRAFTHOUSE

Map 4; 2550 Mission Street, The Mission; ///work.newest.potato;
www.drafthouse.com

Art Deco masterpiece on the outside, hipster dream on the inside, this cinema isn't just for seeing a movie: it's a whole evening of entertainment. Self-professed "ninja servers" stealthily bring food

Try it!
BECOME A FILMMAKER

Always fancied yourself the next Chloë Zhao? Join an Introductory Filmmaking Workshop at the San Francisco Film School *(www.sanfranciscofilmschool.edu)*. It covers everything from screenwriting to editing.

and drink to your seat during screenings (don't try to resist the boozy milkshakes), which tend more toward indie and foreign releases (think awkward masterpiece *Eighth Grade* or South Korea's Palme d'Or-nominated *Burning*). Horror lovers should book a ticket for Alamo's Terror Tuesdays, featuring everything from spooky tales of toxic sheep monsters to seminal Hong Kong thrillers. After the showing, head to the in-house Bear & Bull bar to deconstruct the movie over nitro gimlets.

NEW PEOPLE CINEMA

Map 2; 1746 Post Street, Japantown; ///they.state.lodge; www.newpeoplecinema.com

After something a little different? Or a big fan of Japanese anime? Then add New People Cinema to your bucket list. As the host of various film festivals, this small cinema shows an amazing array of international screenings. Annual events like the Legacy Film Festival on Aging (movies and documentaries about the aging process), the 3rd i (San Francisco International South Asian Film Festival) and CAAMFest (works by and about Asian-Americans) bring an unpredictable and always-brilliant roster of films, in between a regular schedule of anime. This jazzy Japantown cinema (check out the futuristic ceiling and walls) is hidden in the basement of the New People complex, a modern, five-level venue brimming with all things Japanese pop culture.

» Don't leave without browsing the Japan Center shopping mall across the street and popping into the excellent bookstore Kinokuniya to pick up some anime and manga merch.

Spoken Word

*The truest taste of old-style San Francisco can be found
at the city's spoken-word events, where the more
subversive crowd – kink and leather fans, social
justice activists, the radical literati – take the mic.*

POETRY AT THE SACRED GROUNDS

Map 2; 2095 Hayes Street, Haight-Ashbury;
///homes.salsa.vines; 415-387-3859

This cosy mom-and-pop coffeehouse has been around since the
1970s, and so has its Wednesday open-mic night, where amateur and
published poets step up to share their lines. Expect a super-local crowd
of eccentric characters (many of whom first rolled up to the Haight in
1967) and a warm, supportive atmosphere. It's a village-like community, but one populated by a diverse set of funky flower-children.

MORTIFIED LIVE

Map 3; DNA Lounge, 375 11th Street, SoMa;
///frock.palace.faced; www.getmortified.com

Ever read back over your teenage diary and felt utterly mortified by the
words on the page? You're not alone. At this long-running storytelling
night, brave souls take the stage to share embarrassing artifacts of

Sign up to Mortified's newsletter to get advance notice of upcoming events before tickets sell out.

their teenage angst. Love letters and tragic poems are aired for audience amusement, and perhaps some sort of catharsis? Either way, it's cringe comedy at its most hilarious.

MANNY'S

Map 4; 3092 16th Street, The Mission;
///noon.rested.coherent; www.welcometomannys.com

A nightly calendar of Q&As with politicians, activists, journalists, and thought leaders – past speakers include Black Lives Matter founder Alicia Garzer and Speaker of the House Nancy Pelosi – draws a mixed bunch of hippies and hipsters to this civically minded spot. By day, it's MacBooks and macchiatos; by night, spirited debates on hot-button issues like colorism and homelessness. Entry to events is free, but register on the website beforehand.

» Don't leave without trying the food: the kitchen is run by Farming Hope, who train up the homeless and formerly incarcerated.

WRITERS WITH DRINKS

Map 4; Make-Out Room, 3225 22nd Street, The Mission;
///marker.swan.froze; www.writerswithdrinks.com

Authors – local, up-and-coming, and established – read from their latest works (which could be anything from erotica to humorous poems) in this boozy "Literary cabaret." The introductions from host Charlie Jane Anders are as entertaining as the readings, as she ad-libs outrageous bios for each participant before they take to the stage.

OPEN MIC AT CAFE INTERNATIONAL

Map 2; 508 Haight Street, Lower Haight; ///dart.sunset.error; 415-552-7390

Eritrean owner Zahra Saleh is the life and soul of this colorful community hub. Within a couple of minutes of arriving, you'll likely be chatting with her like the regulars, who love the weekly Friday open mics as much as the eye-popping Turkish coffee served here. Expect animated poetry and a live playlist of original tunes from local singer-songwriters.

» Don't leave without chilling on the back patio, where the bright "We The People" mural depicts disparate cultures united by music.

MOAD OPEN MIC

Map 3; Museum of the African Diaspora, 685 Mission Street, SoMa; ///olive.washed.taps; www.moadsf.org

For the SOMA district's "Third Thursdays" free museum and gallery crawl, the Museum of the African Diaspora hosts an evening of spoken word from Bay Area artists of color. Poetry and storytelling pieces tackle anything from feminism to the metaphysics of Blackness, and the crowd tends to represent a cross section of the city.

BAWDY STORYTELLING

Map 3; Verdi Club, 2424 Mariposa Street, The Mission; //starts.crops.boats; www.bawdystorytelling.com

The San Francisco kink community is alive and kicking — and having a fine old time at this monthly storytelling night, where all the true-life tales are about sex. Stories are curated in advance, so you can bet they're all bangers, and are told by a mix of authors, comedians, and regular Joes. The vibe is sex-positive and unintimidating, so come along if you're curious and don't mind a graphic account.

SATURDAY NIGHT AT LA PROMENADE CAFE

Map 6; 3643 Balboa Street, Outer Richmond; ///zones.timing.snacks; www.lapromenadecafe.com

There's such a close-knit vibe around these outer blocks of Balboa Street that they call it "Balboa Village." And this sprawling, vaguely Parisian-style place is at the heart of it all, functioning as a study hall (littered with student laptops and textbooks), secondhand bookstore (all titles $5), and live arts venue. Sure, it's the sort of place where your wine order is "red" or "white," but it's also a wonderfully warm spot to mix with the villagers, especially at the Saturday-night poetry open-mic. First-time poets – this is your chance.

ASIA SF

Map 3; 201 9th Street, SoMa; ///cigar.served.defeat; www.asiasf.com

This is dinner and a show, San Francisco-style. Asia SF has been giving transgender cabaret a platform – or, more literally, a runway – since 1998. The set menu of Pan-Asian food is decent enough, but what you're really here for is a raucous evening of stiff cocktails, free shots, and the all-lip-syncing, all-dancing ladies on the "red dragon runway." It's the Bay Area's premier destination for bachelorette parties, and wallflowers should be warned: these performers can get hands-on.

LGBTQ+ Scene

Although San Francisco's queer bars have taken a hit from high rents and hook-up apps, the scene here still thrives. From leather bars to drag shows, the ultra-risqué to the mega-mellow, there's a night for all tastes.

BEAUX

Map 2; 2344 Market Street, The Castro;
///spared.jazzy.jones; www.beauxsf.com

This joint is pumping on weekends, with punters squeezing in for a spot to live their best lives. The packed crowd – fella heavy, though not female free – is always just-got-paid happy and up for dancing all night long. Things barely simmer down on school nights: see drag shows and the "homo disco circus" on Big Top Sundays, or Cockshot Tuesday's weekly underwear bash.

UHAUL SF

Map 4; Jolene's Bar, 2700 16th Street, The Mission;
///resist.dare.sides; www.uhaulsf.com

If you're not familiar with the term, "getting U-Hauled" is lesbian slang for a relationship that moves super fast (U-Haul is a popular moving company in the US). Gay gals might just find themselves heading down that road at UHAUL, a party at Jolene's Bar every Friday for girls who love girls. The crowd here is cool, diverse, and down to dirty-dance: keep some singles in your back pocket for the ladies busting moves on the bar. Trans, non-binary, and questioning friends are welcome, too.

» Don't leave without making a date to come back on the weekend for Jolene's bottomless brunch.

THE MIX

Map 2; 4086 18th Street, The Castro; ///print.shows.silent; 415-431-8616
The sign outside says "Neighborhood Bar" and that's exactly what you get here. It's about as low-key as can be: no parties or DJs, no puppy masks or drag queens, just a relaxed, no-attitude place to mingle and sip dirt-cheap drinks. The crowd is super-regular – the sort of folks who think of this as a home away from home.

SF EAGLE

Map 3; 398 12th Street, SoMa; ///hours.salads.echo;
www.thesfeagle.com
A storied leather bar with 30-plus years of history, SF Eagle might be the city's premier spot for leather daddies, bears and cubs, pups and handlers, otters and pigs – but it's also super-approachable and chilled-out. Most nights, the large back patio has as many guys clad in plaid as it does in bondagewear, and a decent smattering of ladies, too. The popular regular events are when things get rowdy: see the Sunday barbecue and beer bust, and monthly Growlr parties.

Liked by the locals

"I'm proud that when you come to OASIS, not only are you sitting in the only drag-owned cabaret and club venue of this size, but also, you're not sitting next to a tourist – you're sitting next to locals."

D'ARCY DROLLINGER,
DRAG STAR AND OWNER OF OASIS

OASIS

Map 3; 298 11th Street, SoMa; ///ritual.bless.thin; www.sfoasis.com

The dragstravaganzas in this former gay bathhouse are usually followed by club nights, with DJs spinning tunes 'til 3am. Resident queens are often joined by *Ru Paul's Drag Race* alumni, while Drunk Drag Broadway's kings and queens regularly bring their parody theater: productions include *Man Francisco* and *Sex and the City Live*.

HI TOPS

Map 2; 2247 Market Street, The Castro; ///soak.given.throw; www.hitopsbar.com

This gay sports bar is always poppin', and it's not hard to see why. Between shirtless bartenders, every sport you can imagine playing on a raft of big screens, and a lengthy beer list, it's got everything your sports-loving heart could possibly desire.

LOOKOUT

Map 2; 3600 16th Street, The Castro; ///expand.cakes.clean; www.lookoutsf.com

Drag queens, stiff drinks, and general debauchery, oh my! This lively, two-story watering hole and meeting spot is known for its decked bar – perfect for people-watching – and its no-frills, well-priced drinks. It also functions as a hub for community activities, like letter-writing parties to raise political awareness.

» Don't leave without trying the much-celebrated and oh-so-oozy grilled cheese sandwich.

CASTRO STREET

16TH STREET

STREET

NOE STREET

MARKET

Hit the dance floor at
THE CAFÉ

Drop by the Castro's most poppin' spot, which keeps the LGBTQ+ community and its allies coming back again and again.

*The **Harvey Milk Plaza** was named in honor of the politician in 1985, seven years after his murder. Today it's the heart of the Castro.*

HARVEY MILK PLAZA

17TH STREET

17TH STREET

MARKET STREET

Raise a glass at the iconic
TWIN PEAKS TAVERN

This landmark gay pub is lovely and laid-back. Draw up a chair, sip a pint, and chat with the locals.

DIAMOND STREET

CASTRO

Sashay away to
CASTRO THEATRE

Catch a drag show at the area's namesake historic theater. If you fancy a quieter night, the Castro Theatre also screens movies.

End up at
LA TORTILLA

Soak up the excess with a burrito at colorful La Tortilla, open until 2am.

18TH STREET

CASTRO STREET

Rainbow Honor Walk
remembers figures from the LGBTQ+ community, like Rikki Streicher who ran long-running SF lesbian bar Maud's.

Corona Heights Park

0 meters 100
0 yards 100

19TH STREET

A fabulous night out in
the Castro

San Francisco's famous "gayborhood" has a history of LGBTQ+ activism; this was famously the neighborhood of politician Harvey Milk, the country's first elected official to come out as gay. The Castro has also long been a super-hot spot for a good time, dating back to the 1967 Summer of Love when the LGBTQ+ community partied here. The high jinks haven't dwindled – follow the rainbow flags for a night to remember.

**Dine out at
FRANCES**

Order the tasting menu to appreciate why San Franciscans go wild for this cozy neighborhood bistro (reservations are a must).

1. Frances
3870 17th Street, The Castro; www.frances-sf.com
///chain.colleague.rather

2. The Café
2369 Market Street, The Castro; www.cafesf.com
///firms.public.expect

3. Twin Peaks Tavern
401 Castro Street,
The Castro; www.
twinpeakstavern.com
///items.kind.parade

4. Castro Theatre
429 Castro Street,
The Castro; www.
castrotheatre.com
///copy.pushy.frock

5. La Tortilla
495 Castro Street,
The Castro;
415-861-3990
///artist.beats.bowls

Rainbow Honor walk ///pasta.last.lift

OUTDOORS

Health-conscious San Franciscans love nothing more than being in the great outdoors – walking the city's surrounding trails, exercising in its many parks, and surfing in the bay.

Green Spaces

San Francisco isn't just surrounded by nature; pockets of green punctuate the city. Locals don't take these parks for granted, and woodland strolls and hilltop climbs are popular weekend activities.

GOLDEN GATE PARK

Map 5; Enter at Fulton and 10th Avenue, Inner Richmond;
///civic.mostly.pull; www.goldengatepark.com

Bigger even than NYC's Central Park, this is San Franciscans' oasis. Techies escape the start-up hustle in peaceful redwood groves, while visor-wearing seniors power-walk around Stow Lake. The eastern portion is packed with attractions, from museums to themed gardens, but those in-the-know head for the wilder western half, home to grazing bison and six of the park's ten lakes.

MISSION DOLORES PARK

Map 2; Enter at Dolores and 19th Street, The Mission;
///cool.placed.grab; www.sfrecpark.org

Every weekend is a party at Dolores Park. Here, the young – and young-at-heart – gather under palm trees to flirt, drink, and perhaps even savor a "special truffle" (warning: contains marijuana) from the

Join the fun and buy a West Coast or Japanese craft beer from Dolores Outpost for a picnic date in Mission Dolores Park.

guy hawking them out of swinging copper pots. When Karl the Fog takes a vacation and the sun decides to appear, this is the place to while away an afternoon with SF's partying locals.

ALTA PLAZA PARK

Map 5; Enter at corner of Steiner Street and Clay Street, Pacific Heights;
///smug.remain.galaxy; www.altaplazapark.com

Of course the well-heeled Pacific Heights crowd have a park that looks this grand. Tiered steps at its southern side make Alta Plaza resemble a great Mayan pyramid and grant 360-degree views of the house-dotted hills and bright-blue bay. Instead of a Mesoamerican ruler, it's well-to-do joggers and dog-walkers who puff up these stairs.

» **Don't leave without** soaking up the sunset from here, when the hills and stubby houses are set against a brushed purple sky.

CORONA HEIGHTS PARK

Map 2; Enter at Beaver Street and 15th Street, The Castro;
///torn.beans.brief; www.sfrecpark.org

The mile-long dirt trail that climbs Corona Heights is so steep that Castro locals use the sweat-inducing ascent as their daily workout. At the summit, there's almost always a young couple taking each other's picture on the red-rock outcrop. You won't be able to resist posing for your next profile picture here either, with Downtown San Francisco fanning out behind you, forming the perfect background.

GLEN CANYON PARK

Map 6; Enter at Elk Street and Chenery Street, Glen Park;
///spends.silver.rents; www.sfrecpark.org

Sitting along a deep canyon adjacent to the Glen Park, Diamond Heights, and Miraloma Park neighborhoods, this 70-acre (28-ha) oasis is synonymous with urban trekking. From Monday to Friday, the park is pretty empty except at lunchtime, when workers descend for midday strolls or runs. Come the weekend, almost everyone hits the trails – couples soak up dramatic canyon views, solo walkers come for contemplation, and lycra-clad hiking groups tackle calf-tiring climbs.

THE PRESIDIO

Map 5; Enter at Presidio and Pacific, Presidio Heights;
///sparks.pounds.wheels; www.presidio.gov

It's rare to find a national park so close to residential neighborhoods, but this green space at the foot of the Golden Gate Bridge is just that. Hiking trails wind through thick forest, biking routes trace bayfront promenades, and scenic overlooks show off the soul-

Try it!
GET GREEN-FINGERED

Have a habit of killing off your house plants? Lucky for you, the Presidio Nursery runs workshops where you can learn to grow and care for plants while also doing your bit to help preserve the national park for others.

soaring views that San Franciscans get to see every day. This is where locals come to shout – in their heads, at least – "We live here!" in a rush of self-satisfied glee.

BERNAL HEIGHTS PARK
Map 4; Enter at Powhattan Avenue and Andover Street, Bernal Heights; ///ranged.sleeps.tape; www.sfrecpark.org

You might have to wait for a turn on the tree swing at this park's summit, but generally speaking the gravel trails and views are all yours. And what views they are – taking in everything from the Bayview shipyard at the city's southeastern tip to the western Castro hills. Who needs a tree swing when the vistas on flat ground are this good?

» Don't leave without having a go on the Esmerelda Street Slides, a pair of 40-ft (12-m) metal shoots that are sure to get your legs shaking.

TANK HILL PARK
Map 5; Enter at Twin Peaks Boulevard, Cole Valley; ///action.gums.trail; www.sfparksalliance.org/our-parks/parks/tank-hill

This park more than deserves the moniker of "tank." The hulking 650-ft (200-m) hill serves up one steep grade after the other, all the way to the top of the rocky outcrop. But you'd be hard-pressed to find a better north-facing view of San Francisco anywhere else. With its flat, paved summit – where the eponymous water tank was once located – Tank Hill has become the "it" spot to sit and watch the Fourth of July fireworks. The fact that you can see the pyrotechnics in Crissy Field, Oakland, and the East Bay simultaneously is an added bonus.

Scenic Staircases

There are two things San Francisco has in ample supply: steep hills and jaw-to-the-floor views. This unique topography produces the rare phenomenon of secret, scenic staircases all over the city.

FILBERT STREET STAIRS

Map 1; Montgomery and Filbert, Telegraph Hill; ///empire.muddy.foster

Walking this wooden cliffside staircase is like disappearing into a magical land. As you ascend ever skyward, lush gardens tumble around wood-shingled cottages, bright flowers burst forth over the bannisters, and spindly palms tower overhead. These romantic surroundings are topped off by breathtaking views of the Bay Bridge. If the climb sounds like it'll literally take your breath away, there's no shame in taking it from the top down.

BAKER BEACH SAND LADDER

Map 5; Lincoln Boulevard, between Pershing Drive and Batteries to Bluffs trailhead, The Presidio; ///native.sticky.rider

Beware: in a city characterized by preposterously steep streets, the Baker Beach Sand Ladder is notorious for being quite the workout. It even features as a killer segment of the annual Escape from

Alcatraz Triathlon. Also, the "stairs" – a set of logs and cables careening down a sand cliff – offer limited support to the clumsy-footed. Be sure to rest up at Baker Beach, with its knockout views of the Golden Gate Bridge, before making the climb.

» Don't leave without respecting the nudists on Baker Beach. You don't have to be naked, of course, but be respectful of those who are.

16TH AVENUE TILED STEPS
Map 6; Moraga Street and 16th Avenue, Inner Sunset;
///crib.chins.added; www.16thavenuetiledsteps.com

San Franciscans have started to discover these community-tended stairs and gardens, located in a diminutive little corner of the already rather quiet Inner Sunset. Some people come here for the mosaic tiles, which form a glorious tableau from top to bottom, starting with a sea motif and ending at the stars. Others come for the view looking backward, over the rooftops and out across the Pacific.

After the punishing climb up the 16th Avenue Tiled Steps, you might be tempted to pass on another ascent, but breathe deep and keep climbing. At the crest of the hill, you'll find Grand View Park, one of the only places from which you can see all of the green sweep of Golden Gate Park from above. At sunset, join locals perched among the tree roots on the western side, as the sky over the ocean softens to orange.

THE VULCAN STEPS

Map 2; Ord Street and Vulcan, Corona Heights; ///mats.slang.taking

The best thing about this clandestine concrete staircase is the eclectic collection of houses that it takes in. Residents can only reach their front doors via the 200-or-so steps, so spare a thought for what it's like to bring home the groceries. And how the heck did they manage moving in? We're sure it was worth it for the pleasure of living in this quirky neighborhood, fringed by great thickets of ferns, ivy, and pine; it's practically a poster child for boho SF living.

GREENWICH STAIRS

Map 1; 231 Greenwich Street, Telegraph Hill; ///sings.nearly.back;
www.sisterbetty.org/stairways/greenwichstreet

One of San Francisco's best-kept secrets, the Greenwich Stairs transport walkers to a jungle paradise – it's even advisable to wear bug spray. The steps are fringed by verdant undergrowth and soaring trees, interrupted only by the occasional flap of wings or birdsong. On warm summer days, flocks of San Francisco's famous (and invasive) cherry-headed conures, a species of parrot native to South America, can be heard squawking in the overhead canopies.

LYON STREET STEPS

Map 5; Broadway and Lyon Street, Pacific Heights; ///fruit.hired.update;

The fact that this staircase starts on a street nicknamed "Billionaires Row" tells you everything that you need to know about Lyon Street Steps. The affluent and super-fit locals seem to have mistaken these manicured steps for a StairMaster, but the climb is best appreciated by taking it slow. At the top, the view glides across the bay to mansions scattered across Marin County's ravishingly rugged hills.

» Don't leave without stopping halfway to take in the "Heart of San Francisco" sculpture, part of an annual charitable art installation.

HIDDEN GARDEN STAIRS

Map 5; 1520 16th Avenue, Inner Sunset; ///wooden.ties.busy; www.hiddengardensteps.org

There's no shortage of tiled pieces of public art in SF, but the Hidden Garden Stairs are among the best – and dare we say, the most photogenic. This somewhat secret tiled staircase features flora- and fauna-inspired artworks, shrouded in foliage planted and maintained by an army of local volunteers. The stairs are beautiful at any time of day, but aspiring influencers flock here at Golden Hour, when the waning sun catches the monochromatic tiles and adjacent Victorian buildings in a particularly breathtaking fashion.

EMBARCADERO CENTER STEPS

Map 1; Sacramento and Front streets; ///verge.magic.select; www.embarcaderocenter.com

While not as neon and bright as other scenic staircases in the city, this spiraling staircase boasts jaw-dropping tile work and Brutalist architecture unmatched by any other in San Francisco; you'll wish you had it in your home. Looking down from the top step, the geometric tiles and swirling design almost create an optical illusion.

On the Water

Ringed by its infamous Bay, San Francisco is literally shaped by water and so to are San Franciscans' weekends. From high-octane hijinks to soothing sailing outings, there's something for everyone.

KITE THE BAY

Map 6; 1 Clipper Cove Way, Treasure Island; ///nods.pose.rested; www.kitethebay.com

Captain John is a bit of a legend among newbie kiters. SF's kitesurfing scene is centered on Ocean Beach, where high winds and gnarly Pacific waves are for pros only. But the cap'n takes beginners out into the bay on his support boat, searching out just the right conditions for your skill level. He also uses one-way radio helmets, so he can instruct you as you surf. And, unlike at Ocean Beach, you can even kite-board under the Golden Gate Bridge.

KAYAKING TOURS

Map 3; Pier 40, South Beach; ///galaxy.tribune.rocket

Woken up on a clear morning? A paddle into the bay isn't just gorgeous on a blue-sky day, it's great exercise too. You can go it alone, or join a guided trip on the tough waters under the Bay

If you're a highly experienced kayaker, consider booking a Full Moon or Twilight trip with City Kayak to see the Bay by night.

Bridge or out to Alcatraz Island. Prefer an easier option? Explore gentle McCovey Cove, right by the SF Giants baseball stadium. Its official name is China Basin, but locals renamed it for the Giants player.

SAILING TRIPS

Map 3; Pier 40, South Beach; ///tube.photo.switch

When 25-year-old CEOs need a break from the rat race, nothing blows the cobwebs away quite like sailing on the bay. Weekends see the blue waters surrounding San Francisco chock-a-block with sailboats – big and small – as locals make the most of their home's natural fortunes. Several operators offer day-long, hands-on sailing classes, or, if you're more into total relaxation, skippered charters.

SURFING LESSONS

Map 6; 5000 Pacific Coast Highway, Pacifica; ///bureaucrats.highs.shocking; www.parks.ca.gov

Anyone expecting the quintessential California surfing experience in San Francisco will leave disappointed. The city only has a couple of surf spots, which are both suited solely to the super-experienced. But it's not all bad news. Beginners can drive 30 minutes along the Pacific Coast Highway to Pacifica State Beach, where several surf schools will have you riding waves within the day.

» **Don't leave without** browsing the surfer threads at Nor Cal Surf Shop – the hoodies are practically a mandated uniform in these parts.

Solo, Pair, Crowd

Whether it's meditation, romance, or a party you've got in mind, the Bay is a great place to do it.

FLYING SOLO

Salutations-on-Sea

Find your flow – and test your balance – with a scenic yoga session on a stand-up paddleboard in Richardson Bay. Sausalito's Sea Trek runs several classes a week.

IN A PAIR

Sail at Sunset

Pack a picnic and board a classic schooner for a sunset sail with SF Bay Adventures. Just remember to bring a blanket so you can snuggle away the evening chill.

FOR A CROWD

Toast the Tide

Take a "happy hour" catamaran cruise, complete with bar snacks, around the bay with Adventure Cat or, if your crew's got cash to splash, charter your own.

SEA TREK STAND UP PADDLEBOARD CENTER

**Map 6; 2100 Bridgeway, Sausalito; ///bumps.cube.clock;
www.seatrek.com**

To really bliss out on the water, head across the Golden Gate
Bridge to the little seaside town of Sausalito. Here, families and
friends potter around Richardson Bay – a shallow arm of SF's bay –
on paddleboards, nodding hello to the sea lions and peeking at the
hippie houseboats, which more closely resemble floating cottages.
The view of the San Francisco skyline silhouetted on the horizon is
pretty unforgettable. "Picturesque" just doesn't cut it.

OCEANIC SOCIETY WHALE WATCHING

**Map 5; 3950 Scott Street, Marina District; ///mini.crib.moods;
www.oceanicsociety.org**

Just 28 miles (45 km) off San Francisco's shoreline, there's a collection
of protected islands that are home to both blue whales and great
white sharks. Yes, seeing two of the world's most formidable species
up close is just a day trip away from the city. The nonprofit
conservation organization Oceanic Society runs seasonal, full-day
tours to the Farallon Islands, where these huge marine animals can
be found, but be warned that tickets are pricey and the ride is
rough. For something easier on the wallet (and the stomach), try a
2.5-hour evening cruise to see humpback whales breach under the
Golden Gate Bridge.

» Don't leave without feeling good that your ticket fee funds
educational cruises for under-served Bay Area communities.

Alfresco Fitness

*California's fixation on wellness gets the
San Franciscan treatment with a glut of fun – and
free – group classes in the great outdoors, from
chasing cable cars up hills to yoga on the beach.*

SUNSET YOGA

**Map 5; Baker Beach, The Presidio; ///extend.wisely.plot;
www.outdooryogasf.com**

Outdoor Yoga SF holds alfresco classes at various iconic locations
around the city, but it doesn't get much better than Baker Beach
at sunset. Join the locals for the all-levels vinyasa Sunday session
here or, for something a bit more bonkers than blissed-out, book into
the Friday-night class, which follows up an hour of beach yoga with
an hour of silent disco. Reserve ahead; the fee is $25.

ROOFTOP TAI CHI

**Map 1; Salesforce Park, SoMa; ///tanks.boats.brands;
www.salesforcetransitcenter.com**

There's something very San Franciscan about taking a free tai
chi class in a software-branded public park 70 ft (21 m) in the air.
Located on top of the four-blocks-long Salesforce Transit Center

building, the park is the favorite lunchtime haunt of SoMa's concrete-bound office workers. And, of course, there's nothing to take your mind off your start-up's IPO – or stock market launch – like a spot of afternoon tai chi.

THE GREAT CABLE CAR CHASE

Map 5; 3575 Sacramento Street, Presidio Heights; ///arts.design.scales; www.arunnersmind.com

It's a competitive tech bro's dream. On the last Thursday of every month, fitness shop A Runner's Mind hosts The Great Cable Car Chase, pitting runners against the Powell/Hyde cable car in a two-block uphill race. Meet at the store at 7pm to join the 2.5-mile (4-km) jog to Bay and Hyde streets, where you wait for the next car.

» Don't leave without running back to the shop afterward (assuming you're still alive) for the post-race raffle.

Shh!

Part workout, part social, the Midnight Mystery Ride is the ultimate secret club for keen cyclists. The ride wheels into the night on the third Saturday of every month. First, bag a bike through the Bay Wheels bike-sharing scheme (or book one via the Lyft ride-sharing app) then join the Facebook group, where the starting location is revealed on the day of the ride. Then, follow the leader on a mystery tour through SF's streets, with a few pit stops for beers on the way.

ZUMBA IN THE PARK

Map 5; 198 John F. Kennedy Drive, Golden Gate Park;
///tube.harp.backup; www.sfrecpark.org

There's a free Latin dance party in Golden Gate Park every Sunday at 10am, and everyone's invited. Meeting in front of the carousel at the park's eastern end, a motley assortment of old-timers, eager moms, and good-time students dance it up to the sounds of salsa, reggaeton, cumbia, and merengue. Afterward, follow the moms to the nearby Jamba Juice for a rejuvenating wheatgrass shot.

SUNRISE HILL WORKOUT

Map 5; Alta Plaza Park, Pacific Heights; ///sprint.knee.crazy;
www.november-project.com

If you're the sort of person who gets pumped at the idea of running up a massive hill first thing in the morning, you'll fit right in here. The November Project is an international, free, group-workout community, and the San Francisco chapter just loves those hill repeats, especially at dawn. There are two sessions at Alta Plaza

Try it!
COOK HEALTHY

You've done the workout, now it's time to eat. The Sensitive Foodie Kitchen *(www. thesensitivefoodiekitchen.com)* is run by Karen, a nutritionist, and offers healthy cooking classes with a plant-based focus.

Park on Wednesdays, at 5:30am and 6:30am. It will hurt but, hey, you'll see the sunrise through your tears and you'll have that post-workout glow all day long.

PURUSHA IN THE PARK

Map 6; Golden Gate Park; ///cakes.school.town;
www.purushasevaproject.org

Join the guys and gals who start their Saturday off right with free yoga in the meadow between Queen Wilhelmina Tulip Garden and the Dutch Windmill, at the very western end of Golden Gate Park. Close enough to Ocean Beach to smell the sea air, and surrounded by cypress trees, the setting is well suited to discovering your "true self" – a central pillar of Purusha's holistic style. There's even a sharing circle at the end.

» Don't leave without making a donation to the Purusha Seva Project, which runs free yoga classes for underserved and at-risk groups.

KADAMPA MEDITATION CENTER SF

Map 4; 3324 17th Street, Mission Dolores; ///ocean.cracks.years;
www.meditationinsanfrancisco.org

Suffice to say we could all use a little (or a lot) more calm these days, so a meditation class at Kadampa Meditation Center SF should sit high on anyone's list. All of the center's drop-in meditation classes are perfectly suited for busy urban people, whether they're an exhausted tech worker or continent-crossing traveler. As you might expect from a blissed-out meditation center, it's inclusive and welcoming.

Wonderful Walks

San Franciscans are an outdoorsy bunch. When you live where mountains and forests meet the sea, it's hard to resist getting stuck into nature. So lace up your boots and strike out on one of these great walks.

LANDS END TO BAKER BEACH

Map 6; start at 680 Point Lobos Avenue; ///rocket.badly.film; www.nps.gov

Locals never tire of this spectacular walk, which starts at the mouth of the Golden Gate strait. On sunny weekends, when clear skies show the views at their best, the whole city seems to hit the trail. Follow the sandy path over ocean bluffs and past cypress trees, before emerging in the Sea Cliff neighborhood. From here, take 25th Avenue to end up on windswept Baker Beach.

BATTERIES TO BLUFFS TRAIL

Map 5; start at Lincoln Boulevard, between Pershing Drive and Kobbe Avenue; ///native.sticky.rider; www.presidio.gov

If you're feeling energetic, this is a great add-on to the Lands End to Baker Beach walk, but it's also a dramatic route all on its own. It's short – barely half a mile (1 km) – but challenging, starting with a brutal climb up the Baker Beach Sand Ladder *(p168)* to the trailhead and then following undulating stairways along the steep cliffside. The walk ends at Battery Boutelle, a 20th-century fortification with one hell of a view of the Golden Gate Bridge.

» **Don't leave without** discovering Marshall's Beach, a secluded slip of sand just off the tail that grants perfect photo opportunities.

BAY AREA RIDGE TRAIL

Map 5; start at Arguello Gate, Arguello Boulevard and West Pacific Avenue; ///wake.pans.spots; www.presidio.gov

The Presidio is stuffed with trails, but this 2.5-mile (4-km) route is a local favorite for showing off the best of the park. Starting at the Arguello Gate entrance, it threads through forest and past Andy Goldsworthy's 100-ft (30-m) *Spire* sculpture, before emerging on the coastal bluffs at Pacific Overlook. Here, a reclaimed Monterey cypress-wood bench grants a well-earned rest.

LYON STREET STEPS TO PALACE OF FINE ARTS

Map 5; start at Broadway and Lyon Street; ///fruit.hired.update

This path doubles as a runway for the lucky and loaded who live on "Billionaires Row." Battling them for space on the Lyon Street Steps are puffing runners, who take on the unforgiving incline. The trail stays steep as it traces the edge of the Presidio, before crossing into the Palace of Fine Arts, where amateur artists shelter in the shadows and shade of the Roman-style columns to sketch the scene.

Solo, Pair, Crowd

We all need to gulp in fresh air and watch the world unfold around us. And, handily, San Francisco has a number of great walks for just that.

FLYING SOLO

Contemplative clifftops

Ponder life, the universe, and everything else, as you drink in infinite Pacific views from atop 200-ft- (61-m-) high bluffs on the 2-mile (3-km) Fort Funston loop trail.

IN A PAIR

A sweethearts' stroll

Lover's Lane in the Presidio is the obvious choice for a romantic walk. This path through a eucalyptus grove was once trod by Presidio's soldiers going to meet their sweethearts. Continue on to The Commissary for tapas and cocktails.

FOR A CROWD

Summit with the squad

Conquering the East Peak of Mount Tamalpais, just north of the city, demands the camaraderie of a crew. The 10-mile (16-km) round trip from Bootjack Campground will test your endurance.

FORT MASON TO FORT POINT

Map 5; start at 2 Marina Boulevard; ///hobby.eagles.upper

Discover how the Marina set live on this 3-mile (5-km) waterfront walk. The path ambles along the Marina Green and past the yacht harbor, with its Wave Organ. Then, it's on to Crissy Field, a former airfield that's been transformed into a waterfront park with tidal marshes and picnic areas, before the final stretch to Fort Point.

>> Don't leave without caffeinating up at the Philz Coffee Truck, which is permanently parked on the Marina Green.

THE CASTRO TO TWIN PEAKS

Map 2; start at Castro Street and 19th Street; ///sleepy.gather.dose

This steep urban hike to Twin Peaks' 920-ft (280-m) summit keeps health-obsessed San Franciscans fit. Start on the Castro's main drag, then follow steep residential streets, climbing stairways and alleys past stately Victorians to Crestline Drive. Now, it's time for the final push up to the summit of either Eureka North or Noe South.

MOUNT DAVIDSON

Map 6; start at Dalewood Way and Lansdale Avenue, West Portal;
///sober.police.older; www.mountdavidsoncross.org

Let's set this straight off the bat – a climb up Mount Davidson, the highest peak in San Francisco, is not for the faint of heart. Runners and hikers see the trail, which leads to a large crucifix on the mountain's summit, as a way to test their calves. Foraging for blackberries near the base in fall is a much calmer pursuit.

Nearby Getaways

Of course San Franciscans love their city but sometimes a change of scene and gulp of fresh air is just the ticket. Luckily the city has various tempting day trips right on its doorstep.

POINT REYES NATIONAL SEASHORE

1-hour drive from the city; www.nps.gov

For dramatic coastal hikes, San Franciscans head for this protected shoreline (checking the weather obsessively before they go because fog really spoils the view). After a bracing morning of craggy cliff paths and salty sea air, the one-road town of Point Reyes Station is a lovely stop-off. Sip coffee inside a giant feedbarn at Toby's, then gorge on a hearty sandwich at the Cowgirl Creamery HQ. With your stomach lined, it's time to order a beer at Old Western Saloon, famed for a visit by Prince Charles (there's even a photo to prove it).

» **Don't leave without** touring Heidrun meadery, which produces sparkling, champagne-style meads (fermented honey wine).

SONOMA VALLEY

1-hour drive from the city; www.sonomavalley.com

If Napa is traditional wine country – think expensive restaurants and swanky hotels – then Sonoma is the hipster equivalent. It's where San Francisco's young and restless drink non-interventionist wines under string lights at Scribe Winery, a palm-flanked hacienda. Farm town Healdsburg, an hour's drive north, is the beating heart of the sleeve-tattooed, back-to-the-land scene, where eco-chic boutique hotel h2 tempts environment warriors, and living roof-art galleries tempt creatives from the city. Healdsburg even has a seasonal ice-cream and pie bar called Noble Folk.

Try it!
FORAGE FOR FOOD

Sonoma isn't just about wine. ForageSF hosts "wild food walks" searching out seaweed, mushrooms, and more along the Sonoma coastline, with the guidance of an expert forager *(www.foragesf.com)*.

MUIR WOODS NATIONAL MONUMENT

30-minute drive from the city; www.nps.gov

This ancient forest of towering, old-growth redwoods feels worlds away from the hubbub of San Francisco. So, come the weekend, those craving the great outdoors don their hiking boots and set off on the 90-minute loop of the sun-dappled forest floor. Mount Tamalpais State Park is right next door if they're craving a longer hike.

TIBURON

30-minute ferry ride from Fisherman's Wharf; www.destinationtiburon.org

It may not be as popular as other coastal towns on the northern side of the Golden Gate Bridge, but those in-the-know head to Tiburon, which is just as beautiful. Take in the panorama from Shoreline Park, which stretches from Downtown SF's high-rises to the green of the Presidio. Make a beeline for Sam's Anchor Cafe, and get a seat on the deck: oysters and a glass of Chardonnay just taste better with that view.

VALLEJO

1-hour ferry ride from San Francisco Ferry Building; www.visitvallejo.com

Down-to-earth San Franciscans love Vallejo precisely because there's no "scene." It's just a sleepy little town that's firmly off the tourist trail. But boring, it is not: take the downtown Art Walk, where local artists sell their works on the sidewalk on alternate Fridays, and the volunteer-maintained wetlands of the Mare Island Preserve.

» Don't leave without sipping a small-batch brew on the sunny patio of the Mare Island Brewing Company's Ferry Taproom.

NAPA VALLEY

1.5-hour drive from the city; www.visitnapavalley.com

Okay, it's the playground of retired hedge fund managers who think that owning a vineyard would make a good hobby. But for San Franciscans – financiers or otherwise – Napa Valley is a glorious escape from city life. Small-town St Helena, surrounded by rows of vines, is the ideal combination of ritzy and relaxed. Browse the cute boutiques on Main Street, then sip a flight at the Clif Family Winery tasting room, while grazing on a bruschetta from the on-site food truck.

SAUSALITO

20-minute drive from the city; www.visitsausalito.org

It's a classic with locals and visitors alike. So, no, you might not be alone as you cross the Golden Gate Bridge to the gorgeous bayfront town of Sausalito. But that hardly matters when the views from this side of San Francisco Bay are that astonishing. Be sure to continue on to Richardson Bay, where you'll find the hippie houseboat communities that inspired Otis Redding's "(Sittin' On) The Dock of the Bay."

PACIFICA

20-minute drive from the city; www.visitpacifica.com

"Pacifica" means peaceful in Spanish, and this perfectly sums up this oceanfront community, which has an unpretentious vibe that's all about reconnecting with the simpler stuff. That might be surfing Pacifica State Beach (home to the most scenic Taco Bell), hiking up Sweeney Ridge, or strolling the rugged bluffs at Mori Point.

An afternoon exploring
Golden Gate Park

We get it; at 3 miles (5 km) in length, and with more acres than NYC's Central Park, San Francisco's most famous green space can seem a bit daunting. After all, it's got museums, lakes, conservatories, botanical gardens, a bison paddock, polo fields – the list goes on. So where do you begin? The best way to attack it: have a plan. We suggest walking end to end, and stopping at just a few select spots to get a sense of what makes Golden Gate Park every San Franciscan's favorite pleasure garden.

1. Stow Lake and Strawberry Hill
50 Stow Lake Drive East; www.stowlakeboathouse.com
///level.called.statue

2. Disc Golf
99 Marx Meadow Drive; www.sfdiscgolf.org
///ever.mason.alert

3. Dutch Windmill
1691 John F. Kennedy Drive
///steer.fever.tamed

📍 **de Young Museum**
///melt.frock.grit

📍 **Polo Fields**
///flips.flops.belong

📍 **Spreckels Lake**
///brass.solid.brass

Be transported by the DUTCH WINDMILL
Never been to the Netherlands? Stop by the windmill and tulip garden, and you'll feel like you have. After, grab dinner and drinks at Beach Chalet next door.

Lincoln Park

Land's End

LINCOLN WAY

JUDAH STREET

GREAT HIGHWAY

PARK PRESIDIO BLVD

25TH

19TH

GEARY   BOULEVARD

AVENUE

AVENUE

RICHMOND

Spreckels Lake *was added in 1904 for model boating enthusiasts; today the "Spreckels Irregulars" meet here regularly to race.*

The **de Young Museum** *was rebuilt after the 1989 earthquake and clad in copper so that, when it oxidizes, it will turn green to echo its gardens.*

Tee off at
DISC GOLF

You don't need to be a pro to enjoy a putt around. Gulp in fresh air as you swing your way around the park's golf course.

FULTON   ST

JLTON   ST

Bison Paddock

Japanese Garden

Polo Fields

Golden Gate Park

Savor the scenery from
STOW LAKE AND
STRAWBERRY HILL

Rent a paddleboat for an hour or so before climbing the mid-lake island for a picnic at the top.

San Francisco Botanical Garden

LINCOLN   WAY

The **Polo Fields** *might be busy with soccer players (rather than polo) but in 1967, this is where the Summer of Love's gatherings often took place.*

27TH

19TH

INNER SUNSET

SUNSET

KIRKHAM   STREET

AVENUE

AVENUE

BOULEVARD

SUNSET

NORIEGA   STREET

0 meters   500

0 yards   500

With a little research and preparation, this city will feel like a home away from home. Check out these websites to ensure a healthy, safe stay in San Francisco.

San Francisco
DIRECTORY

SAFE SPACES

SF is often ranked the most liberal city in the US, but should you feel uneasy at any point or want to find your community, there are spaces catering to different sexualities, demographics, and religions.

www.sfcenter.org
LGBTQ+ community center providing resources and services.

www.sfhsa.org
List of local community centers.

www.transgenderlawcenter.org
Trans-led advocacy organization providing programs and support.

www.womensbuilding.org
Historic community center offering social and advocacy services for at-risk women.

www.ywamsanfrancisco.org
Features a map of SF's religious spaces.

HEALTH

Health care in America isn't free, so it's important to take out comprehensive health insurance for your visit. If you do need medical assistance, there are many pharmacies and hospitals across the city.

www.healthright360.org
Collection of affordable community health care clinics and services.

www.sfcityclinic.org
Low-cost sexual health clinic, including emergency contraception and post-exposure medication to prevent HIV.

www.sfdph.org
A complete list of local clinics from San Francisco Department of Public Health.

www.walgreens.com
Store locator showing 24-hour and late-night Walgreens pharmacies.

www.zuckerbergsanfrancisco general.org
Inpatient, outpatient, and emergency care for all, regardless of insurance.

TRAVEL SAFETY ADVICE
Before you travel – and while you're here – always keep tabs on the latest regulations in San Francisco, and the US.

www.sanfranciscopolice.org
Safety tips, precinct news, and inform- ation on how to report various crimes.

www.sfnightministry.org
Multi-faith nonprofit providing referral services, counseling, and a crisis helpline.

www.sf.gov
COVID-19 news and advice from the City and County of San Francisco.

www.stopaapihate.org
Website for reporting hate crimes against the Asian American and Pacific Islander communities.

www.travel.state.gov
Latest travel safety information.

www.twitter.com/sf_emergency
Real-time safety alerts.

ACCESSIBILITY
Most venues in San Francisco do a good job of being accessible, as do surrounding state beaches and parks. These resources will help make your journeys go smoothly.

www.accessnca.org
Guide to accessibility for attractions, and accommodations here in Northern California.

www.access.parks.ca.gov
Database and map of accessible features in California state parks.

www.luxorcab.com
Accessible taxi services, with the same meter rate as standard taxis (see also Yellow Cab and Town Taxi).

www.sfmta.com/accessibility
Official guide to public transportation for people with specific requirements, from SF's transportation agency.

www.wheelingcalscoast.org
A wheelchair user's guide to the California coast, covering beaches, parks, and trails.

ABOUT THE ILLUSTRATOR

Mantas Tumosa

Creative designer and illustrator Mantas moved from his home country of Lithuania to London back in 2011. By day, he's busy creating bold, minimalistic illustrations that tell a story – such as the gorgeous cover of this book. By night, he's dreaming of adventures away, catching up on the basketball, and cooking Italian food (which he can't get enough of).

Main Contributors Matt Charnock, Laura Chubb

Senior Editor Lucy Richards

Senior Designer Tania Gomes

Project Editor Zoë Rutland

Project Art Editor Bharti Karakoti

Editors Elsepth Beidas, Rebecca Flynn, Lucy Sara-Kelly

Proofreader Kathryn Glendenning

Senior Cartographic Editor Casper Morris

Cartography Manager Suresh Kumar

Cartographer Ashif

Jacket Designer Tania Gomes

Jacket Illustrator Mantas Tumosa

Senior Production Editor Jason Little

Senior Production Controller Stephanie McConnell

Managing Editor Hollie Teague

Managing Art Editor Bess Daly

Art Director Maxine Pedliham

Publishing Director Georgina Dee

First edition 2021

Published in Great Britain by Dorling Kindersley Limited, DK, One Embassy Gardens, 8 Viaduct Gardens, London SW11 7BW, UK.

The authorised representative in the EEA is Dorling Kindersley Verlag GmbH. Arnulfstr. 124, 80636 Munich, Germany.

Published in the United States by DK Publishing, 1450 Broadway, Suite 801, New York, NY 10018.

Copyright © 2021 Dorling Kindersley Limited
A Penguin Random House Company
21 22 23 24 10 9 8 7 6 5 4 3 2

A NOTE FROM DK EYEWITNESS

The world is fast-changing and it's keeping us folk at DK Eyewitness on our toes. We've worked hard to ensure that this edition of San Francisco Like a Local is up-to-date and reflects today's favourite places but we know that standards shift, venues close, and new ones pop up in their place. So, if you notice something has closed, we've got something wrong or left something out, we want to hear about it. Please drop us a line at travelguides@dk.com